THE BRISTOL SUFFRAGETTES

THE BRISTOL SUFFRAGETTES

LUCIENNE BOYCE

SilverWood

Published by the author in 2013
using SilverWood Books Empowered Publishing ®

SilverWood Books
30 Queen Charlotte Street, Bristol, BS1 4HJ
www.silverwoodbooks.co.uk

Copyright © Lucienne Boyce 2013

ISBN 978-1-78132-106-5

British Library Cataloguing in Publication Data
A CIP catalogue record for this book is available from the British Library

Set in Sabon and Univers by SilverWood Books
Printed by Berforts Group Ltd on responsibly sourced paper

"Remember the dignity of your womanhood. Do not appeal, do not beg, do not grovel. Take courage, join hands, stand beside us, fight with us."

Christabel Pankhurst

"We are here not because we are law-breakers; we are here in our efforts to become law-makers."

Emmeline Pankhurst

Contents

Introduction

In October 1903 Mrs Emmeline Pankhurst (1858–1928) founded the Women's Social and Political Union (WSPU) in the drawing room of her house in Manchester. Its aim was to win women the vote on the same terms as it was or would be granted to men. From its modest beginnings it grew into a national organisation with well-equipped headquarters in London and an annual income of thousands of pounds. A new word was coined to describe the bold women who carried out its tactics: suffragettes.

The WSPU was not the only suffrage organisation and not all campaigners for the female franchise agreed with the militant methods it used in its attempt to force the Government to grant votes for women. Those who preferred constitutional methods are usually known nowadays as suffragists. Many of them were represented by the National Union of Women's Suffrage Societies (NUWSS), which was formed by a combination of local groups in 1896.

The dispute about whether or not the female franchise owes more to the suffragettes or suffragists is a complex one. Probably the answer lies somewhere in-between. That the WSPU did make an impact is not in question however. At the very least, they got the women's suffrage campaign, so long overlooked by politicians and ignored by the press, noticed.

This book tells the story of the Bristol branch of the WSPU and some of the women who worked for it in the cause of votes for women. It also includes a map and walk for those of you who would like to explore the Bristol of the suffragettes.

Bristol and the Suffragettes

From the outset one of the WSPU's main campaign aims was to make the movement a national one. Their goal was "the organisation of women all over the country to enable them to give adequate expression to their desire for political freedom".[1] In 1906 there were three branches; by 1907 there were fifty-eight. Bristol was soon added to their number. The largest city in the South West, it was the obvious centre for the expansion of the movement across the region.

Bristol also had a long-established culture of female political campaigning, stretching back to the anti-slavery campaign (the Bristol and Clifton Auxiliary Ladies Anti-Slavery Society was formed in 1840), and the suffrage campaigns of the 1880s. Bristol women had been actively involved in local and national campaigns for the education of women, women workers' rights, housing reform, and the co-operative movement. Many of the veteran suffrage campaigners played a part in the establishment of the WSPU in the city, as will be seen later.

Bristol was also firmly in the grip of the Liberals, the party in power throughout the suffragette campaign. The WSPU's policy of opposing any government which refused to grant the vote to women meant that this was of especial significance. Three of the city's four MPs were Liberals, two of them were Government ministers, and one of those mnisters was a prominent anti-suffragist.

Bristol was thus an important focus for the WSPU's national campaign. It attracted major figures in the movement to make speeches and lobby Government MPs, and it was in Bristol that some of the most significant events of the campaign took place.

Differences of Opinion

As with any political or social campaign, the suffrage movement was divided by ideology and method. Some of the main areas of debate were:

- Were militant tactics right or effective?
- Should married women have the vote?
- Should the franchise campaign focus on universal adult suffrage rather than votes for women?

- Should there be a property qualification?
- At what age should women have the vote?
- Should suffrage organisations be run on democratic principles? (The NUWSS and Women's Freedom League (see page 38) were democratic organisations; the WSPU was not.)
- Should the suffragists work within political parties? (The WSPU severed ties with all political parties, including the Labour Party. The NUWSS worked for many years with the Liberal Party until in 1912 it formed an alliance with the Labour Party.)

And, of course, there were the anti-suffragists – men and women who did not think women should have the vote at all.

The Women's Social and Political Union

WSPU membership was open to women only. The new organisation adopted the motto "Deeds not words" and distanced itself from any political party, arguing that none of them had shown any practical commitment to their cause. The Pankhurst family's own political background was in the socialist movement. Mrs Pankhurst was the widow of radical lawyer Dr Richard Marsden Pankhurst (1835/6–1898), and with him she had joined in earlier campaigns for the women's franchise. Dr Pankhurst's death left his family in straitened circumstances and when Mrs Pankhurst set up the WSPU she was working as registrar for births and deaths in Chorlton to support herself and her four children: Christabel (1880–1958), Sylvia (1882–1960), Adela (1885–1961) and Henry Francis (Harry) (1889–1910), who was named after a brother who died at the age of four in 1888.

Women had been campaigning for the vote for fifty years. They had lobbied MPs, sent petitions to the House of Commons and promoted the cause in speeches, pamphlets and newsletters. These early campaigners relied on Private Members' Bills to bring about the reform, but none of them had succeeded because they lacked government backing. Since what was needed was a government measure, Mrs Pankhurst decided that pressure must be put on the government. The WSPU would oppose any government which refused to give women the vote. At the outset suffragette militancy took the form of heckling government MPs and ministers, and campaigning against their candidates at by-elections.

According to Christabel Pankhurst, the first militant action was on 20 February 1904 when, braving the hostility of the gathering, she raised the issue of votes for women during a Free Trade League meeting in Manchester addressed by Winston Churchill (1874–1965), the Liberal MP for North West Manchester. There was no scuffle with the police, she was not ejected from the hall, and she did not go to prison. What made her action militant was that a woman had invaded a male political space and forced the question of votes for women upon its attention. The incident was mentioned in *The Guardian.*

Unfortunately, it was quickly forgotten and Christabel decided that more drastic action should be taken to get her point across. She determined that next time she would have an answer to her question – or go to prison. On 13 October 1905 she and her friend, Annie Kenney (1879–1953), who was to become a key figure in the WSPU, went to a Liberal meeting, also in the Free Trade Hall. There they asked Edward Grey (1862–1933) and Winston Churchill if the Liberals, who were expected to win the next general election, would give women the vote. The women were ejected. Outside, Christabel Pankhurst committed what she termed a technical assault against a police officer (she spat at him) and thus obtained their arrest. She was sentenced to seven days in prison, and Annie Kenney three.

The incident was also reported in the press, as was the subsequent demonstration in Manchester to protest against the Liberals, which was held on the day of Annie Kenney's release. Churchill wrote to *The Guardian* (2 November 1905) to refute charges that the women had been roughly treated, and accused them of undemocratic behaviour for disrupting the meeting. For the first time in years, the WSPU felt, women's suffrage was news. It showed that getting arrested was a useful way of generating publicity for the cause, as well as attracting recruits and embarrassing the Government. From now on WSPU members would follow Christabel Pankhurst's and Annie Kenney's example and deliberately risk arrest.

By 1907 Mrs Pankhurst had resigned from her job, given up her home, and become a full-time campaigner for women's right to vote. Mrs Pankhurst's eldest daughter, Christabel, finished her law studies in Manchester in June 1906 and joined her mother in London. The WSPU established its London headquarters at 4 Clement's Inn, and appointed Emmeline Pethick-Lawrence as Treasurer. With her wealthy husband, Frederick (1871–1961), Mrs Pethick-Lawrence founded and financed the WSPU newspaper, *Votes for Women*. The WSPU structure was in place and the organisation was ready to grow. One of its next steps was to establish itself in Bristol.

The Suffragettes Come to Bristol

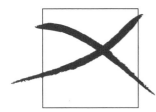

In 1907 Annie Kenney arrived in the city to found the Bristol and West of England branch of the WSPU. Annie, a former mill-girl and trade unionist from Lancashire, was one of the WSPU's stars and a loyal follower of Emmeline and Christabel Pankhurst. Following her three days in prison in 1905, she was again detained in March 1906 after knocking on the door of 10 Downing Street, though she was not charged. She served a second, six-week term of imprisonment after being arrested in June 1906 during a deputation to Herbert Asquith's house in London's Cavendish Square. She was one of ten women sent to Holloway after a demonstration in the Central Lobby of the House of Commons at the opening of Parliament on 23 October 1906.

Annie Kenney already had experience of setting up a WSPU office, having been instrumental in establishing their headquarters in London. Then she had turned for help to Mrs Pankhurst's second daughter, Sylvia, who had to give up her studies at the Royal College of Art in Kensington to concentrate on the WSPU campaign. Annie's other helpers included Labour MP Keir Hardie (1856–1915) and suffrage campaigners Isabella Ford (1855–1924) and Flora Drummond (1879–1949). Isabella Ford was a Labour activist who withdrew from the WSPU when it severed relations with the Labour Party. Flora Drummond went on to become a WSPU organiser and was arrested on many occasions.

Annie stayed in a series of lodgings, eventually settling for a while at 23 Gordon Road, Clifton (Number 1, Walk). As she had in London, she relied on the support of local activists in carrying out her task. There was already a long tradition of involvement in the women's suffrage movement in the city. The Bristol and Clifton branch of the National Society for Women's Suffrage was formed in 1868, and later affiliated to the NUWSS. During the 1870s they organised speaking tours in Bristol, Bath and the South West, held meetings on the Downs, in the Colston Hall and the Victoria Rooms; held drawing-room meetings in Clifton and Redland; collected signatures on petitions; and circulated women's suffrage journals and pamphlets.

Annie Kenney

Many Bristol women took part in other feminist struggles: the campaign for the Married Women's Property Acts (allowing married women to own property in their own right); the repeal of the Contagious Diseases Act (which made prostitutes suffering from venereal disease in naval and military towns liable to incarceration in hospitals); the reform of divorce laws; and the provision of higher education for women. In addition, a number of Bristol suffragists were involved in England's first Women's Liberal Association (WLA), which lobbied Liberal MPs for support for the women's franchise.

It was to this formidable group of campaigners that Annie Kenney turned. In her autobiography she remembered in particular the help she was given by "Miss Priestman and Miss Colby".[2] The Quaker sisters, Anna Maria (1828–1914) and Mary Priestman (1830–1914), who moved to Clifton from Newcastle in 1869, were both prominent in the Bristol suffrage society. In the 1870s Anna Maria was Secretary of the Ladies' National Association for the Repeal of the Contagious Diseases Acts and helped form the National Union of Women Workers in Bristol. It was she and Emily Sturge (1847–1892) who in 1881 founded the Women's Liberal Association. The Priestman sisters were not strangers to non-legal protest, having previously refused to pay their taxes in protest at women's unenfranchised position. Both made donations to the WSPU.

Maria Colby was an organiser for the NUWSS in Bristol. In the early 1880s she organised a number of meetings on the Downs. She also wrote a poem protesting against the idea that women's main duty was to darn their husband's stockings, which was so often and so tediously put forward as an argument against giving them the vote.

The Priestman sisters' niece, Lilias Ashworth Hallett (1844–1922), a Bath Quaker who was a founding member of the Bristol and Clifton National Society for Women's Suffrage, was a well-known speaker for the suffrage cause. She gave generous sums of money to the WSPU. On 13 February 1907 she joined a WSPU deputation to the House of Commons, where she was arrested but released. She attended a welcome breakfast for released WSPU prisoners in 1908, and chaired a meeting at Eagle House, Batheaston, in May 1908, when Annie Kenney spoke.

Mrs Agnes Beddoe (c.1832–1914), one of the founders of the Bristol and Clifton National Society for Women's Suffrage and a WLA member, gave money and attended WSPU meetings. Her husband became Vice President of the Bristol Men's League for Women's Suffrage, which was founded in 1907 and supported the WSPU and the Women's Freedom League (see page 38 for the WFL).

Other local women who were already members of the NUWSS in Bath or Bristol joined the WSPU. One of them was Clara Codd (1876–1971), who moved to the new organisation in 1907 after hearing Annie Kenney give a talk. She became Annie's assistant, organising and speaking at meetings. In 1908 she was appointed Honorary Secretary of the Bath branch of the WSPU. On 13 October 1908 she was arrested during a demonstration at the House of Commons and served a month in Holloway. She was said to be the first Bath woman to suffer imprisonment for the cause.

Mary Blathwayt (1879–1961) joined the WSPU in July 1906, though she remained a member of the NUWSS until 1908. She became Treasurer of the Bath WSPU in 1908 and worked with Annie Kenney in Bristol. She chalked pavements and handed out leaflets, ran the Bristol WSPU shop, arranged meetings, went to some of the London demonstrations, and chaired outdoor meetings. For a time Mary lived with Annie Kenney in Bristol lodgings, and did her washing and mending for her.

Annie also brought a helper from WSPU headquarters: Aeta Lamb (1886–1928). Aeta had been a member of the WSPU since 1906 and took part in WSPU deputations to the House of Commons, which resulted in two terms of imprisonment in Holloway. Her duties in Bristol included helping to organise meetings, one of which was the first WSPU meeting in Bath on 1 April 1907.

Mrs Pankhurst's youngest daughter, Adela, came to Bristol in the summer of 1908 before moving on to take up the post of WSPU organiser in Yorkshire that autumn after giving up her teaching job. Like her sister Sylvia, Adela remained committed to the Labour movement, which their mother Emmeline and elder sister Christabel rejected. The family's political differences eventually led to the expulsion of both Sylvia and Adela from the WSPU some years later.

There was much coming and going of temporary workers like Adela, many of whom volunteered to spend their holidays helping the campaign in the South West. Annie was known by them as "our Captain" and she spoke enthusiastically about the Bristol workers: "How splendid the women are," she reported in *Votes for Women* on 11 June 1908, "it is wonderful to see them rise to every call that is made."

The Blathwayts of Batheaston

Mary Blathwayt was the daughter of Colonel Linley Blathwayt (1839–1919), who retired to Eagle House, Batheaston, in 1882 after serving in India, and his wife Emily (1852–1940). The Blathwayts were among the WSPU's most ardent West Country supporters. Eagle House became a place where suffragettes could rest and recuperate after speaking tours or prison sentences.

Colonel Blathwayt, whose interests included natural history, photography, and gardening, had the idea of inviting his suffragette guests to plant trees to commemorate their visits. He established "Annie's Arboretum", most of which has now been built over. Each planting ceremony was recorded in photographs taken by the Colonel. Annie Kenney; Christabel, Adela and Mrs Pankhurst; and Mrs Emmeline Pethick-Lawrence were frequent guests and planted trees at Eagle House. So too did many of the women mentioned in this book, including Theresa Garnett, Lillian Dove-Willcox, Clara Codd, Vera Wentworth and Aeta Lamb.

Mary never took part in any militant activities, though the Blathwayts' Batheaston friends, Grace and Aethel Tollemache and Mrs Cave, were militants. A third Tollemache sister, Mrs Everett, and their mother, Mrs Tollemache, also supported the WSPU.

It was to be the intensification of militancy that eventually led to the Blathwayts' withdrawal from the WSPU. Mrs Blathwayt resigned in 1908 and Mary in 1913, when local houses were targeted by arson. However, the Blathwayts remained interested in the cause of women's suffrage. When the First World War broke out they joined the Bath Red Cross Society. Mary died at Eagle House on 25 June 1961.

All three Blathwayts kept diaries which recorded many details of the campaign in the south-west, the famous suffragettes they met, and the militant exploits of their friends. Many of their observations are quoted in this book. You can see Colonel Linley's photographs of the suffragettes on the Bath in Time website www.bathintime.co.uk.

A Liberal City

After the Liberal Party's landslide victory in the 1906 elections, a government was formed under Prime Minister Herbert Henry Asquith (1852–1928), who was opposed to votes for women. The WSPU's strategy of harassing the Government was to have significant repercussions for Bristol. The MPs for Bristol North, South and East were Liberals, and two of them were Cabinet ministers.

Sir Charles Edward Henry Hobhouse (1862–1941)

Charles E H Hobhouse was the Liberal MP for Bristol East from 1900 to 1918. As an active anti-suffragist, he was a figure of both local and national significance in the suffrage campaign. The WSPU was to quote one of his Bristol speeches as a direct incitement to extreme militancy (see page 45). He was a Church Estates Commissioner between 1906 and 1907; Parliamentary Undersecretary for India 1907–1908; and Financial Secretary to the Treasury between 1908 and October 1911. In 1911 he entered the Cabinet as Chancellor of the Duchy of Lancaster, a post he held until 1914. He was Postmaster General from 1914 to 1915, during the development of wireless telegraphy. He supported free trade and Irish home rule.

Augustine Birrell (1850–1933)

Augustine Birrell was elected Liberal MP for Bristol North in 1906. He trained as a barrister and was Professor of Law at University College London between 1896 and 1899. He also wrote essays on literature and was an enthusiastic book collector. He was Chief Secretary for Ireland from 1907 to 1913. For the last years of his Irish tenure he struggled to cope with his second wife Eleanor's illness. He made several attempts to resign but these were rejected by Prime Minister Asquith. Eleanor's brain tumour caused insanity and her death in 1915. Having been blamed for the Dublin Easter Rising, Birrell retired from politics in 1916.

Sir William Howell Davies (1851–1932)

Welsh-born Sir William Howell Davies was Liberal MP for Bristol South from 1906 to 1922. He was Chairman of the Bristol Docks Committee from 1899 to 1908, and of the Bristol Finance Committee from 1902 to 1929. He was knighted for his municipal services in 1908.

George Abraham Gibbs (1873–1931)

George Abraham Gibbs was the Conservative MP for Bristol West from 1906 to 1928. A former soldier, he was Party Whip between 1917 and 1928, and Treasurer of the Royal Household between 1921 and 1928. Gibbs lived at the Gothic mansion of Tyntesfield just outside Bristol, which had been built out of the family fortune founded on the trade of guano, a fertiliser made from bird droppings. (The National Trust acquired Tyntesfield in 2002; this magnificent mansion is well worth a visit. For details see www.nationaltrust.org.uk.)

Campaigning in Bristol

By July 1908 a temporary WSPU shop and office had opened at 33 Queen's Road. The shop proved so successful that permanent premises were taken at 37 Queen's Road (Number 5, Walk) in April 1909.

> *We have a list of all our meetings in one window, and in the other the big photo of Mrs Pankhurst in the centre. In the glass door we have our* Votes for Women *poster – we show our pamphlets and books, display our colours and scarves, ties, ribbons, etc. in the big window. Inside we have our banners and our literature beautifully set out on nice shelves around the shop...Miss St John and Miss Blathwayt are the ones who have done the decorating of the shop.*
>
> Annie Kenney describes the shop at 33 Queen's Road
> *Votes for Women* 30 July 1908

Expansion in the South West was rapid. By 1909 there were organisers based in Plymouth, Penzance and Torquay. In 1910 a WSPU shop and office opened in Bath at 12 Walcot Street (since demolished).

From their Queen's Road base, the Bristol suffragettes organised fund-raising activities such as jumble sales and Self-Denial Week; pavement chalking and poster parades to advertise meetings; and street sales of the WSPU newspaper *Votes for Women*. There was an impressive programme of meetings in and around Bristol, Bath and the West Country. Speakers were often key WSPU figures such as Emmeline and Christabel Pankhurst, and Emmeline Pethick-Lawrence. In fact, WSPU speakers were never in one place for long. Annie Kenney herself was often away from Bristol on speaking tours and attending demonstrations.

Many meetings were held in the open air. Favourite spots included Bristol Quay, the Horsefair and Blackboy Hill. Annie Kenney and others also spoke in Portishead, Clevedon and on the beach at Weston-super-Mare. There were visits to parks around Bristol and regular meetings on the Downs. Annie Kenney recorded run-ins with Liberal supporters who came to interrupt their meetings, and also noted the "educated hooligans" who came along to heckle them on the Downs in August 1908.[3]

A major event was the rally on Durdham Down on 18 September 1908. Mrs Pankhurst, Christabel Pankhurst and Mrs Emmeline Pethick-Lawrence were among the speakers. The meeting was advertised by pavement chalking and a wagonette with banners which was driven around the city. A number of open-air meetings were held in the days leading up to the rally. Between six and seven thousand people were reported to have attended. Interrupters with their "bells and tin whistles" were soon persuaded to disperse, no doubt influenced by the "strong, athletic-looking young fellows...displaying the [WSPU] Union's favours" who had come along to protect the speakers.[4] A suffrage resolution passed at the meeting was sent to Asquith and Bristol MP Augustine Birrell.

Meetings were held outside factory gates. There were dinner-hour meetings in the factories around Portland Square and outside the Wills Tobacco Factory in Bedminster. Annie Kenney noted the number of unemployed men who attended lunchtime meetings on the Horsefair: "They listen most attentively, and mutter 'Sorry, Miss', when we go round with the collecting tin".[5]

The women were constantly at risk of violence from the crowds. In Bristol on 8 June 1909, Mary Blathwayt was hit by potatoes, stones, turf and dust, and Elsie Howey's lip was cut. During her talks, Bristol suffragette Victoria Lidiard was pelted with soggy bananas, accosted by drunken sailors, and reprimanded by angry clergymen.

Popular indoor venues included the Victoria Rooms (Number 4, Walk), where for a meeting on 3 April 1908, Aeta Lamb hired six professional boxers to protect the speakers after Bristol medical students threatened to break up the gathering. Afternoon at-homes were held weekly in the Hannah More Hall on Park Street (Number 6, Walk). They would typically begin with tea at 3.30pm followed by a speaker at 5 pm. Others were scheduled in the evenings to give working women a chance to attend.

The at-homes soon grew so popular that they moved to the Victoria Rooms. The Colston Hall (Number 9, Walk) was a key venue for major events: Mrs Pankhurst and Christabel Pankhurst often spoke there.

Social evenings and tea parties were held at supporters' homes. The Blathwayt family offered Eagle House for a garden party at which Annie Kenney spoke on 23 May 1908. Mrs Cuthbert Hicks, who, with Phyllis Smale, ran a drama school in Durdham Down, lent her garden at White Lodge, Coombe Dingle, for the sale of cakes and sweets. One member gave a suffrage dinner at which she covered the lights with Votes for Women scarves; displayed purple, white and green flowers; and headed the menu cards "Taxation and Representation should go together. Taxation without representation is Tyranny".[6]

Activities were not confined to local events. On 13 June 1908 six or seven thousand women, many of whom were professional women and graduates, marched from the Embankment to the Albert Hall in a demonstration organised by the London Society for Women's Suffrage. A number of organisations took part in the rally, including the NUWSS, the Artists' Suffrage League and the National Union of Women Workers. The WSPU were not officially involved in the event, but WSPU members were encouraged to attend. Some West Country women travelled to London and special trains were laid on from Bristol, Bath and Weston-super-Mare.

A few days later, on 21 June, the WSPU held its own demonstration. Their Chelsea procession alone numbered 7,000 women, and the rally doubled or even tripled its anticipated attendance of 250,000. Twenty special trains brought supporters from the provinces, among them a West Country contingent. Mary Blathwayt, in white muslin, helped carry the Bath banner, and Annie Kenney spoke at one of the twenty platforms in Hyde Park.

The WSPU thought that their meeting fulfilled the Government's demand for evidence that there was a popular demand for the female franchise. In fact, they believed that it was the largest political gathering ever held – although *The Times* suggested on 22 June that many people went simply out of curiosity. Nevertheless, what the suffragettes saw as a mandate to give women the vote failed to move the Government. Christabel Pankhurst accordingly announced that the next WSPU meeting in London's Caxton Hall on 30 June 1908 (the fourth in a series of meetings that were known as the Women's Parliament) would consider the women's next move.

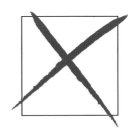

Opposite Page

Here during Self-Denial Week in 1910, Bristol suffragettes raise money. From left to right: Edith West, Mary Allen, Miss Staniland, Elsie Howey, Mrs Dove-Willcox. WSPU Treasurer Emmeline Pethick-Lawrence introduced Self-Denial Week in 1908 as a fund-raising activity. Members were sent collecting cards, and raised money by street collections, selling jewellery, donating a day's pay, whist drives, or holding drawing-room concerts in their homes.

The Women's Parliament

The first Women's Parliament was held on 13 February 1907 in London's Caxton Hall and set the precedent for subsequent gatherings. At the end of the meeting the women marched to the House of Commons to protest against the omission of the women's franchise from the King's speech. In accordance with WSPU policy, they were prepared to be arrested in the attempt. Fifty-four women were detained, and two men. During the struggle to get through the police lines, they met with such brutal treatment from the police barring the approach to the House that the police were lampooned in the press as "London Cossacks".

According to the WSPU leaders, it was the Government's stubborn refusal to respond to peaceful tactics such as petitions and asking questions at meetings, coupled with the increasing brutality of the treatment meted out to the suffragettes during national and local demonstrations, that led to the escalation of suffragette militancy.

Stone-Throwing and Starvation

By the time of the fourth Women's Parliament the routine of deputations and arrests was well established. So too was the violent treatment the demonstrators suffered at the hands of police and male bystanders. Being arrested was often the only thing that saved women from serious injury in the streets, for once they were in police custody they were removed to the safety of the cells. However, on the evening of 30 June 1908, a marked police reluctance to make arrests exposed women to rough handling on an unprecedented scale.

When Mrs Pankhurst set off with the first deputation, which Prime Minister Asquith had, as usual, refused to receive, Parliament Square was full of police and crowded with spectators. At intervals other small deputations followed the first group. In their attempt to reach the House, women were dragged off down side streets and subjected to physical and sexual assaults. So infuriated were Mary Leigh and Swindon-born Edith New by the violence, they went to 10 Downing Street and threw stones through the windows. Their action was not undertaken on instructions from WSPU leaders. However, it was later endorsed by Mrs Pankhurst, who said, "The smashing of windows is a time-honoured method of showing displeasure in a political situation."[7]

This unsanctioned act of two angry women was adopted as official WSPU policy. At the eighth Women's Parliament, on 29 June 1909, the first organised window-smashing targeted government offices. The stones were wrapped in the deputations' undelivered petition to Asquith. One hundred and eight women, including Mrs Pankhurst, were arrested. The women were freed pending an appeal hearing in December. The appeal was in due course dismissed, and the women paid their fines. However, twelve of them had been charged with window-breaking and they were sentenced and sent to Holloway. They broke the windows in their stifling cells, were put in solitary confinement, and embarked on a hunger strike.

The Hunger Strike and Forcible Feeding

In late 1908 WSPU leaders Mrs Pankhurst, Christabel Pankhurst and Mrs Flora Drummond were imprisoned in connection with handbills distributed by the WSPU asking the public to help them "rush the House of Commons" on 13 October. After her release from prison in December, Mrs Pankhurst insisted on the women's right to be regarded as political prisoners. She directed that from now on all WSPU members should refuse to obey prison rules.

In June 1909, artist and illustrator Marion Wallace Dunlop (1864–1942) was arrested after stencilling pro-suffrage graffiti on a wall at the House of Commons. With Mrs Pankhurst's directions in mind, she went on hunger strike after being refused political prisoner status and was released after ninety-one hours. Other suffragettes were soon emulating Dunlop's action. Prison doctors were forced to release hunger-striking women on health grounds. Thirty-seven women evaded their sentences in this way. Determined to put a stop to this, the Government introduced the forcible feeding of prisoners in September 1909.

Among the Holloway twelve were Bedminster-born widow Lillian Dove-Willcox, Mary Allen (WSPU organiser in Newport and Cardiff) and Leeds suffragette Theresa Garnett. The group was released after a few days. In the House of Commons Herbert Gladstone accused them of violent behaviour against prison wardresses.

On 29 July the twelve women were at a meeting in London to receive medals from Mrs Pankhurst when a police inspector arrived to serve summonses on Dove-Willcox and Garnett. Each faced two charges of assaulting wardresses during their stay in Holloway. Theresa Garnett was accused of biting one of the prison officers. This case was dismissed when it was suggested that the "bite marks" came from the WSPU portcullis brooch she had been wearing, and which was torn off her blouse during a struggle to remove her from her cell. On the other charge she was sentenced to one month in prison.

Lillian Dove-Willcox was sentenced to a ten-shilling fine or ten days on one charge, and a forty-shilling fine and ten days on the other; sentences to run concurrently. She opted for imprisonment. Back in prison both women were put into punishment cells. They were released on 8 August 1909 after a hunger strike.

On 4 September Lillian Dove-Willcox and Mary Allen returned to Bristol. Mary Blathwayt was among the banner-carrying women who formed a welcoming procession led by Annie Kenney that met them at the railway station. Unfortunately, the band that had promised to play ducked out at the last minute, but WSPU member Violet Bland decorated the garden at her house in Henley Grove, Henleaze, where she ran a domestic science college, for their reception.

Militancy in Bristol

In 1909 Asquith and his Government set out on a tour of Britain to promote the "people's budget" and to challenge the House of Lords' right of veto. The Lords had blocked the budget, which would increase taxation of the wealthy, and other government legislation, including bills on education and plural voting. To protect the politicians from the suffragettes, women were banned from meetings and speakers were guarded by large contingents of police. The Liberals, however, underestimated the resourcefulness and determination of the WSPU militants.

Bristol North MP Augustine Birrell was accosted at Bristol Temple Meads Railway Station by Elsie Howey (organiser for Paignton and Torquay) and Vera Wentworth (organiser for Plymouth) in March 1909. "Tut tut," he said in response to their demand for the vote. He was probably tutting again in the Colston Hall on 1 May 1909 when Elsie Howey and Vera Holme interrupted his speech on land taxes with cries of "Votes for women!" They had spent the afternoon hiding in the organ, from where they watched police search the building before the meeting started. Other women, armed with a megaphone, protested outside the hall from a rented room in a nearby house. Vera Holme later commemorated the escapade in a poem in which she hoped, rather optimistically, that "…Mr Birrell/Daren't speak in that hall again/And it may be, never in Bristol, Until the vote we gain!"[8]

On 3 July Birrell and his wife attended Sir Herbert and Lady Ashman's garden party at Cook's Folly, their house in Sneyd Park overlooking the Avon Gorge. Birrell was due to speak in support of the budget. As he and other guests went through the gates they were given suffrage leaflets by women, but the meeting was not interrupted.

In November, Winston Churchill, then President of the Board of Trade, came to Bristol. Churchill was giving a series of speeches, later published as *The People's Rights*, in which he criticised the House of Lords and Conservatives for rejecting the "people's budget". He had been invited to address the 140th meeting of the Anchor Society at the Colston Hall on Saturday 13 November.

The Anchor Society was a charitable organisation founded in memory of eighteenth-century Bristol merchant Edward Colston (now largely remembered for his involvement in the slave trade rather than as a founder of schools and almshouses in the city). The Society was then open about its involvement in Liberal politics, but nowadays is apolitical.

In the days leading up to Churchill's visit, the Bristol WSPU circulated leaflets reminding readers that the 1832 Bristol Riots had been instrumental in the passing of the Reform Act the same year which broadened the male franchise. The leaflet invited women to assemble "in their thousands" outside the Colston Hall. The day before Churchill arrived, Nurse Pitman of Clifton "sent a message to Mr Winston Churchill".[9] The message was half a brick, and it was delivered through the plate glass windows of the Post Office in Small Street. Mary Allen broke the windows at the Board of Trade's office in Baldwin Street, and Vera Wentworth attacked the Liberal Club windows. The next morning Wentworth and Allen were sentenced to fourteen days in prison and Nurse Pitman, who had caused more damage, was listed for trial on the following Wednesday. Vera and Mary went on hunger strike when their demand for political prisoner status was refused by the Governor of Horfield Jail and were forcibly fed.

On Saturday afternoon Churchill alighted from the Paddington train in Temple Meads Railway Station to find that instead of cordial handshakes from the Anchor Society, it was "rough treatment from Theresa Garnett".[10] Garnett, who was staying at 5 York Place in Clifton (Number 2, Walk), broke through the cordon of Bristol detectives surrounding the politician and lunged at him with a whip crying, "Take that you brute!" She told the police her name was "Votes for Women" before being dragged away to be charged with assault. The charge was later changed to disturbing the peace and she was sentenced to a month in Horfield, where she went on hunger strike and was forcibly fed. She protested by setting fire to her cell and was placed in solitary confinement. She was later moved to the prison hospital.

Churchill, who was accompanied at the Colston Hall by Augustine Birrell, received what he called a more "kindly welcome" that evening.[11] Only a few minutes into his speech a heckler reminded him that "women have been tortured by the Liberal Government".[12] The man was ejected. Churchill, referring to the power of the electorate to defeat the Lords by voting out the Conservatives, waxed lyrical about the "voting powers which their fathers won for them in the past, which they value so highly at present, and which they are bound in honour to hand on uninjured to their children's children".[13] Meanwhile Nurse Pitman, Vera Wentworth, and Mary Allen were singing suffragette songs in their cells and perhaps reflecting on their struggle for a vote to hand down to their daughters.

The WSPU held its own Colston Hall meeting a few days later, on 24 November 1909. According to Mary Blathwayt, hundreds of students rushed the platform and threw flour over Christabel Pankhurst and Annie Kenney. Another woman was struck in the face and badly injured.

Criticism of the WSPU

The non-militant NUWSS had initially been sympathetic to suffragette tactics. After the demonstration in the Central Lobby of the House of Commons on 23 October 1906, Millicent Garrett Fawcett (1847–1929), its President, wrote to *The Times* on 27 October in defence of the arrested women. She criticised the press's reporting of the incident. While stressing the NUWSS's intention to continue its constitutional campaign, she credited the suffragettes with bringing the question of votes for women to the nation's attention. As Mrs Pankhurst was herself to do so many times, she laid the blame for militancy on the politicians who refused to pay attention to the women's demands. She crowned this public declaration of support by giving a banquet for the prisoners on their release.

The NUWSS attitude changed after the first unofficial stone-throwing on 30 June 1908. Mrs Fawcett continued to praise the suffragettes' courage and self-sacrifice, and was still doing so in her 1920 reminiscences of the campaign. However, she felt that June 1908 marked an abandonment of the principle that the women themselves should bear the brunt of any suffering arising from militancy. In spite of acknowledging the organisations' shared aim, she deplored the use of violence and firmly disassociated the NUWSS from the WSPU.

As militant actions increased, many WSPU members who had either left the NUWSS or held joint membership of both organisations moved back to the constitutional campaign. Among them were the Priestman sisters of Clifton. Lilias Ashworth Hallett also grew critical of militancy.

Some members disliked militancy but remained in the WSPU; Aeta Lamb was one of these. Many others left. In September 1909 the Union lost one of its staunchest West Country supporters when Mrs Blathwayt resigned. She blamed stone-throwing and the use of personal violence against politicians, and in particular an assault on Asquith. The Prime Minister was accosted by Elsie Howey, Vera Wentworth and Jessie Kenney, Annie Kenney's sister, on 5 September 1909 in Lympne, Kent. They surrounded him outside church and struck him, and in the evening threw stones through the window of Lympne Castle where he was dining with his wife and other guests. Christabel Pankhurst supported their actions, and an unrepentant Vera Wentworth told Mrs Blathwayt that if the Prime Minister continued to refuse to receive suffrage deputations "they will pummel him again".[14]

A Women's Anti-Suffrage League was formed in 1907, and novelist Mary Humphry Ward (whose novels *Delia Blanchflower* and *The Testing of Diana Mallory* promoted the anti-suffragist view) became its President in 1908. In June 1909 Mrs Humphry Ward announced that the League already had 15,000 members, 110 branches, and 320,000 people had signed its anti-suffrage petition. In 1910 the organisation merged with the Men's League for Opposing Women's Suffrage to form the National League for Opposing Women's Suffrage.

The anti-suffragists argued that the majority of women did not want the vote, but regarded it as a burdensome responsibility. Some feared the break-up of family life if women's energies were directed away from the home. Many argued that women were incapable of understanding politics or making decisions affecting the Empire, and since they did not engage in the defence of the nation they should not have the right to vote. Others feared that the inversion "of the natural role of the sexes" would make Britain incapable of resisting the "manly" Germans.[15]

Splits in the WSPU

Differences within the WSPU resulted in three major splits:

The Women's Freedom League

The WFL was formed in 1907 by women who left the WSPU over a disagreement about the undemocratic constitution favoured by Emmeline and Christabel Pankhurst.

East London Federation of Suffragettes

Later known as the Workers' Suffrage Federation, the ELFS was founded by Sylvia Pankhurst in 1912. The East London Federation was part of the WSPU until 1914, when Sylvia was expelled following disagreements with Emmeline and Christabel Pankhurst over her socialism and her campaign among working women in the East End.

The United Suffragists

In October 1912 Mr and Mrs Pethick-Lawrence were expelled from the WSPU following disagreements with Emmeline and Christabel Pankhurst about escalating militancy. The Pethick-Lawrences retained the WSPU newspaper *Votes for Women*, while the WSPU produced its own newspaper, *The Suffragette*. In 1914, with other former WSPU members, the Pethick-Lawrences formed the United Suffragists, an attempt to unite militants and non-militants, to which they gave the newspaper *Votes for Women*.

Truce, Pageants and Plays

In 1910 an all-party Conciliation Committee was established with the aim of promoting a franchise bill acceptable to all. In order to facilitate its work the WSPU halted militancy, though it continued its by-election campaigning during the general election in early 1910. Truce did not mean an end to suffrage activity, and meetings and demonstrations in support of the bill continued in London and the rest of the country.

Mary Blathwayt and her friends, Mrs Tollemache and Grace and Aethel Tollemache, were among the suffragettes who marched behind the Bath banner at a colourful women's procession on 18 June 1910. The procession – the day after mourning for King Edward VII ended – included women from the professions as well as militant and non-militant organisations. Mrs Pankhurst led the 617-strong prisoners' group, who were clothed in white. Dr Garrett Anderson, pioneer of women in the medical profession, led a contingent of university women. They marched to the sound of forty bands, and the march ended with a meeting in the Albert Hall.

While the WSPU and other suffrage societies continued to rally support for the bill the antis were also busy. On 28 June Hobhouse called a meeting with Anti-Suffrage League leader Lord Cromer, Conservative and Unionist MP Austen Chamberlain, and Cabinet Minister Lewis Vernon (Lulu) Harcourt. Hobhouse was appalled by their lack of response to the threat of the Conciliation Bill. He commented: "The Anti-Suffrage Women's Assoc [*sic*] certainly justified their refusal to accept the responsibility of the vote by exhibiting a state of do-nothingness and incapacity which was typical of women's capacity to do serious work."[16] The first anti-suffrage Trafalgar Square demonstration was held on 16 July. The anti-suffragists also sent out a questionnaire to women ratepayers in a number of cities, including Bristol.

In Bristol a novel event organised by the local WSPU was the matinee performance of Cicely Hamilton's *A Pageant of Great Women* and her one-act play, *How the Vote Was Won*. These were staged at the Prince's Theatre on 5 November 1910. Prince's, which opened in 1867, stood on Park Row (Number 12, Walk) and was destroyed during a German bombing raid on 24 November 1940.

PRINCES THEATRE, BRISTOL.

A Pageant had premiered at the Scala, London, in 1909. In the play a host of famous women from history – including Joan of Arc, Sappho, and Jane Austen – challenge male prejudice by demonstrating women's achievements as artists, heroes, rulers and saints.

Hamilton's plays were among the many suffragette dramas sponsored by the Actresses' Franchise League (AFL), whose members included Ellen Terry, Lena Ashwell, Lillie Langtry and Sybil Thorndike. The AFL lent its support to non-militant and militant suffrage campaigners. For the performance in Bristol many parts were taken by local women. WSPU member Victoria Lidiard played Queen Victoria in *A Pageant*. Mrs Cuthbert Hicks and her husband had parts, and Lillian Dove-Willcox and Alice Walters appeared in *How the Vote Was Won*. They acted alongside theatre and WSPU stars like Edith Craig as Rosa Bonheur and suffragette Lady Constance Lytton (1869–1923) as Florence Nightingale. During the interval, cups of "votes for women tea" and biscuits were sold.

This Page
Cicely Hamilton, the author
of *A Pageant of Great
Women*, as Christian Davies.

Opposite Page
Prince's Theatre, Park Row.

Resisting the Government: Tax and Census

Many women refused to pay their taxes in protest against women's unenfranchised position and a Women's Tax Resistance League was formed in 1910. Among the West Country resisters was the Blathwayts' friend, Mrs Tollemache of Batheaston Villa. Her goods were auctioned at the White Hart in Batheaston in 1911, 1912 and 1913, and purchased by sympathisers who promptly returned them to her. At the last sale, suffragettes carrying "No Vote, No Tax" banners protested outside during the auction.

Another opportunity for non-violent resistance to the Government came with the census on 2 April 1911. The WFL and WSPU organised a women's boycott, arguing that "if we don't count, we refuse to be counted". Women were encouraged to spoil their census form or spend the night away from home so that the census officials could not include them on their returns.

Bath WSPU organiser Mrs Mansel took a house at 12 Lansdowne Crescent where local evaders spent the night. Mary Blathwayt was one of the twenty-nine women who slept there. Among the entertainments they enjoyed was a lecture on clairvoyance, and music performed by sisters Aethel and Grace Tollemache. In Bristol, Annie Kenney spent the night at 9 Whatley Road. The census enumerator noted on her form that Annie refused to complete it, though under occupation she did put "suffragette".

Birrell Takes to His Bed

The first Conciliation Bill, based on a property qualification which would enfranchise about one million women, was introduced on 14 June 1910. It passed its second reading but when the Government refused to give it further facilities, a WSPU deputation was sent to the House of Commons by the ninth Women's Parliament on 18 November 1910. In Parliament Square they met with violence from police and bystanders on such a scale that the day became known as Black Friday. In retaliation, the WSPU truce was broken over the next few days by window-smashing at 10 Downing Street, the House of Commons, the Home Office and other Government buildings. One hundred and seventeen women and two men were arrested but subsequently released without charge.

On 23 November Augustine Birrell cancelled a meeting in Bristol and took to his bed, saying he had been assaulted by suffragettes during continuing disturbances in London the day before. Christabel Pankhurst denied that he had been injured by WSPU women, and said he had himself told a journalist that he twisted his knee when walking. Whatever the nature of his encounter with the suffragettes, the police's search for someone to prosecute came to nothing.

The WSPU renewed its truce when a second, redrafted Conciliation Bill was presented. However, they continued their by-election campaigning during the December general election. Hobhouse was elected in East Bristol for the fourth time on 4 December by an increased majority.

The redrafted Conciliation Bill passed its second reading in May 1911, but again the Government refused to give it further facilities. Instead, Asquith announced on 7 November that a Government manhood suffrage bill would be introduced in the next session, which would be capable of amendment to include women. It meant the end of the Conciliation Bill, which could not succeed without Government support.

On 17 November 1911 Asquith promised a deputation of suffrage societies that if either the Conciliation Bill or the Government Reform Bill was approved by a majority in the

Commons, the Government would give facilities for it to pass into law. Although other delegates had confidence in Asquith's pledge, the WSPU thought it was a trick and brought the truce to an end.

The WSPU held a Women's Parliament at Caxton Hall on 21 November 1911. Mrs Pankhurst was on a lecture tour of America and in her absence Emmeline Pethick-Lawrence led a deputation to the House of Commons. It was accompanied by organised window-breaking at Government buildings, including the War Office, Home Office and Foreign Office. Two hundred and twenty women and three men were arrested, among them Bath suffragettes Mrs Cave, Mrs Mansel and Aethel Tollemache. Aethel was sentenced to fourteen days' imprisonment, where she was fed the vegetarian diet of bread, milk, eggs and butter.

Cabinet ministers were again heckled mercilessly at meetings. Annie Kenney led a demonstration at Bath Skating Rink on 24 November where Lloyd George was speaking about franchise reform at a meeting of the Liberal Federation. There were police barriers around the door of the rink and women were excluded from the meeting. Nothing daunted, she addressed the crowd from a nearby roof using a megaphone. Meanwhile, a number of male supporters in the hall interrupted Lloyd George. Manchester suffragette Mabel Capper (1886–1966) was arrested for breaking Bath Post Office windows and sentenced to imprisonment for a month.

In January 1912 Mrs Pankhurst returned to England. On 16 February 1912, at a meeting in London to welcome Mrs Pethick-Lawrence and others released from Holloway after the November 1911 demonstration, Mrs Pankhurst announced that the WSPU would resume "the argument of the stone". She added ominously that they would not use any stronger methods, provided this was sufficient. A demonstration was announced for 4 March and the WSPU started its preparations, collecting stones and distributing hammers to volunteers to use for breaking windows.

Hobhouse Lights a Fuse

On the day that Mrs Pankhurst made her speech, Hobhouse addressed a meeting of the National League for Opposing Women's Suffrage in the Colston Hall. Other speakers were Lord Cromer and Mrs Humphry Ward, who described the Bristol branch of the League as one of the strongest in the country. Admission was by ticket, issued on the condition that holders did not interrupt the proceedings. The hall was protected by uniformed and plain-clothed police, and Hobhouse was escorted from Temple Meads by Scotland Yard and local detectives.

The evening opened with an organ recital, and when Hobhouse began to speak, one of the first interruptions came from the back of the stage. A London suffragette had locked herself in the organ loft; she was soon ejected. In his speech, punctuated by cries of "Hear, hear!", "Rubbish" and "Votes for women", Hobhouse argued that there was no mandate from the country to give women the vote. He pointed out that pro-suffrage candidates had not been successful at elections. What was more, while the suffragettes could organise "noisy demonstrations…they had not had in the case of the suffrage demands the kind of popular sentimental uprising which accounted for Nottingham Castle in 1832 or Hyde Park railings in 1867".[17] (Nottingham Castle was attacked by arsonists in protest at the Duke of Newcastle's opposition to parliamentary reform, and the Hyde Park railings were torn down by campaigners for male suffrage.) He suggested that the nation's opinion, which he believed to be against female suffrage, could be ascertained by a referendum.

At question time Hobhouse was quizzed further about the referendum by a woman wearing a Votes for Women ribbon. Then, from the top tier of seats, Lillian Dove-Willcox pressed the issue, causing an uproar and an unsuccessful attempt to remove her. When order was restored she demanded, "Are you willing to submit Home Rule or Welsh Disestablishment to a referendum?" Her efforts to ask further questions were drowned out by votes of thanks to the speakers and she was ejected from the hall. She left in a tram car waving to her cheering supporters.

Mrs Pankhurst seized on Hobhouse's speech (and similar speeches by other politicians) as a justification of militancy. She reminded the public that the violence in "the very city in which Mr Hobhouse made his speech" led directly to the passing of the 1832 Reform Act.[18] It was Hobhouse's speech, she said, which led to the militants' decision "to nerve ourselves to do more".[19] As far as Sylvia Pankhurst was concerned, Hobhouse's words were like "a match to the fuse".[20]

The Argument of the Stone

Mrs Pankhurst had announced that a demonstration would take place on 4 March 1912. While the police were still making plans for dealing with it, she launched an unannounced window-smashing raid on 1 March. She led a group of women who broke windows at 10 Downing Street and was arrested with them. For the next hour, fifteen-minute relays of women broke windows in Haymarket and Piccadilly. After a lull in the proceedings windows were broken in Regent Street and the Strand. This was followed by an attack on the windows of Oxford Circus and Bond Street.

On the morning of 4 March more women stepped up with their stones and hammers. The windows of Knightsbridge shops were broken, and that evening, windows in post offices, government buildings and ministers' houses were damaged. Grace Tollemache was one of two hundred women arrested during the demonstrations. She was sentenced to two months' hard labour in Holloway. Bristol suffragette Victoria Lidiard received the same sentence for breaking a window at the War Office. During her imprisonment, her sisters kept her spirits up by shouting messages from the street.

Mrs Pankhurst was also sentenced to two months' imprisonment. The police raided WSPU headquarters on 5 March and Christabel Pankhurst fled to Paris. From there she continued to direct the movement and edit *Votes for Women*.

On 28 March a third Conciliation Bill came up for a second reading and was defeated. Many laid the blame on WSPU militancy. On 8 April Mrs Pankhurst was released from prison on bail, her window-breaking sentence remitted. Instead she faced trial on 15 May, with Mr and Mrs Pethick-Lawrence and Mabel Tuke (1871–1962), for conspiracy to damage property. On 22 May sentences of nine months' imprisonment were handed down. Their demand for political prisoner status was refused and they were released in June after a hunger strike.

In July Christabel Pankhurst started a campaign of secret arson attacks. Hobhouse was among the first to be targeted when an attempt was made on his home in Corsham, Wiltshire, which burned down the back door. In the same month the Government introduced its own Reform Bill, as notified by Asquith on 7 November 1911. There was no provision for votes for women.

In October Mr and Mrs Pethick-Lawrence left the WSPU after a disagreement over the increasingly violent militant tactics. They retained *Votes for Women*, which the WSPU replaced with *The Suffragette*. As soon as they had gone, on 17 October, Mrs Pankhurst announced the new campaign: "There is something that Governments care more for than human life, and that is the security of property...I incite this meeting to rebellion."[21] From now on, private as well as government property was to be attacked by the militants in the belief this would put added pressure on the government to meet the women's demands.

Mrs Pankhurst later characterised the years 1907–11 as "Peaceful Militancy".[22] Now Peaceful Militancy was over. Instead she had started "The Women's Revolution".[23]

A Royal Visit

On 28 June 1912 King George V, accompanied by Queen Mary, came to Bristol to open the King Edward VII Memorial Infirmary. The new 520-bed facility was funded by a War Office scheme and was intended for military use should the need arise.

After spending the morning in Cardiff, the King and Queen arrived at Temple Meads Railway Station at 1.45 pm. In rain and hailstorms they went to Clifton College and the Council House, and then to the new Infirmary. Bristol MPs Hobhouse and Birrell were in attendance, as was the Home Secretary, Reginald McKenna (1863–1943). It was a holiday in the city, and among the events organised to welcome the visitors were a twenty-one gun salute on Durdham Down and a living Union Jack formed by 2,500 schoolchildren.

The suffragettes had also prepared welcoming parties. McKenna was accosted in Llandaff by London suffragette Helen Craggs, who jumped over a wall, grabbed his arm, and had to be hauled off him by the police. She later denounced McKenna for "jaunting about the country while women were starving in prison".[24] In Temple Meads Miss Billings, a well-known militant, waited for the arrival of the King and Queen. Whatever her plan had been, it was thwarted when she was recognised and bundled into one of the station offices before the Royal party's train arrived. After they had safely passed into the city she was sent back to London on the next train.

Bristol and the Women's Revolution

By the end of 1912 the Women's Revolution was under way. In November there was a five-day campaign of letter box attacks around the country, and letter boxes in Bristol and Bath were targeted. False fire alarms were raised and there were some arson attacks. In line with Mrs Pankhurst's direction that no human life was to be endangered, properties selected for arson attacks had to be empty, and also isolated in order to allow the arsonettes to escape. However, in the New Year Mrs Pankhurst again called a halt to militancy pending the debate on the women's suffrage amendment to the Government's Reform Bill.

When this bill also failed, the third WSPU truce ended in unprecedented destruction. Telephone wires were cut, pillar boxes damaged, works of art vandalised, boathouses and sports pavilions set alight, the tea house in Kew Gardens was burned by Bristol suffragette Lillian Lenton, empty houses were set on fire, and golf courses attacked. Ministers received letters laced with pepper or snuff. Hobhouse was among the victims of these postal pranks and the fact that he was a hay fever sufferer won him much sympathy. "Dummy" bombs were left on the London Underground and in public buildings, while real ones wreaked havoc.

As more women were sent to prison, the Government had to admit that forcible feeding was not having the desired effect of keeping them in prison to serve out their sentences. The women endured long hunger strikes and forcible feeding to the point where their health broke down and they had to be released from prison or die: they were still evading their sentences. In the House of Commons MPs asked "Should we let them die?" The feeling was that, popular though this option might be, they could not allow it. The Government responded to the crisis by rushing through The Prisoners (Temporary Discharge for Ill-Health) Act – the notorious "Cat and Mouse Act". Under this legislation, hunger strikers could be released on licence to recover from their ordeal, but would be rearrested to continue their sentences when they had recuperated. The power to forcibly feed prisoners was retained.

The Government was now determined to break up the WSPU. Mrs Pankhurst was sentenced to three years' penal servitude on

2 April 1913 on a charge of incitement to commit a felony. She immediately embarked on a gruelling cycle of hunger, sleep and thirst strikes, release, and rearrest which lasted until 1914. The WSPU was prohibited from holding outdoor meetings, the printers of *The Suffragette* were arrested, WSPU headquarters were frequently raided, and other WSPU leaders were put on trial. *The Suffragette* sub-editor, Laura Lennox, was sent to Horfield to serve her six-month sentence, where she went on hunger strike. She was released under the Cat and Mouse Act and rearrested in Shirehampton.

For the first half of 1913, however, Bristol was relatively calm. The local WSPU organised harmless events such as weekly at-homes, outdoor meetings and debates. On 5 March there was a discussion about militant methods at the Liberal Association Room in Fishponds. Members ran social evenings, cake sales and jumble sales. Fund-raising received its usual annual push with Self-Denial Week in March. There was a performance of Evelyn Glover's suffragette comedy *A Chat With Mrs Chicky* at the Co-operative Hall in Fishponds. The only hint of the Government's ferocious struggle with the WSPU leadership came in May after a raid on WSPU London headquarters, when local sales of the prohibited newspaper *The Suffragette* soared.

The heckling of local MPs continued. South Bristol MP Sir William Howell Davies was interrupted during a meeting in April and several men and women were ejected. On 27 June Augustine Birrell addressed a meeting at the Colston Hall on Home Rule. He was interrupted by male suffragists, who were violently ejected. One man was thrown down stairs and two women had their clothes torn.

On 4 July King George was in Bristol again, this time to view the statue of Edward VII outside the Victoria Rooms and to attend the Royal Show on Durdham Down. As his carriage was travelling along Park Street, London suffragette Mary Richardson ran out of the crowd and tried to drop a petition onto his knees. One of the riders flanking the vehicle wheeled round and hit her with the flat of his sword. She was arrested, but the police had difficulty getting her away from the hostile crowd. One woman slapped her

King George V Raising his Hat to the Statue of his Father. July 4th 1913.

face, and another struck her on the head with an umbrella. The police hustled her onto a tram and took her to Bridewell Police Station. She was later released without charge at the King's request.

It was not until October, however, that Bristol witnessed its most spectacular disturbances. Once again Hobhouse seemed to have goaded the suffragettes to action. Mary Richardson had been arrested, with Rachel Pease, on 14 October 1913 and charged with setting fire to a house in Hampton-on-Thames. At a meeting about Ireland in Bristol on 22 October, Hobhouse was interrupted by demands for Richardson's release. He said that he was hostile to votes for women and hoped the measure would never pass. The WSPU's response was swift. In the early hours of Thursday morning, 23 October, the University Sports Pavilion at Coombe Dingle, completed only two years previously at a cost of £2,000, was destroyed by fire. Suffragette literature was found nearby and a note on a black-edged envelope: "Business before pleasure. Hobhouse being responsible will pay. Release Mary Richardson".

MORE ARSON BY WILD WOMEN.

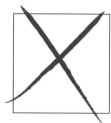

This Page

The burnt-out University of Bristol Sports Pavilion, *Daily Mirror* 26 October 1913.

Opposite Page

King George V views the statue of his father, Edward VII, outside the Victoria Rooms, 4 July 1913. Suffragette Mary Richardson attempted to drop a petition into his carriage as it went up Park Street.

The students were as swift to retaliate, and when lectures ended on Friday 24 October they met to plan their response. Their decision was soon made and they armed themselves with bricks, sticks, hatchets and a basket of inflammable materials which they dragged down to the WSPU shop at 37 Queen's Road. Meanwhile, someone warned the two women who were in the shop about the imminent attack, and they telephoned the police who promised them protection.

There were around three hundred students, who split into two groups. At 5pm they converged on the shop. They smashed their way in, looting and wrecking all the way to the office upstairs, where they threw a typewriter out of the window. They sent the roll-top desk after it. Within eight minutes the shop was a wreck, traffic was at a standstill, and a bonfire fuelled by books, furniture and papers taken from the premises blazed in the street. One of the women in the shop escaped through a back door, but for her companion the only way out was by jumping from an

upstairs window. She landed without injury and both got away.

The promised police protection did not arrive. There was only one policeman on duty nearby, at the top of Park Street, when the attack began. When officers eventually arrived on the scene they did nothing more than keep the crowds out of harm's way. Indeed, the students had so little to fear from the constabulary that on Saturday morning, when women were seen going into the shop to start clearing up, they launched a second attack. They pelted the women with missiles and eggs, and once again drove them out through the back door and an upstairs window (there was a ladder available this time). They smashed what little remained, attempted to light another bonfire, and overpainted the "Votes for Women" sign with "Varsity".

This time the police did stop them lighting the bonfire, but the only arrest made during the two days was of a student who assaulted a police officer on Saturday. Superintendent Halsall, who was in charge of the Clifton police, said that they could not make arrests: "The thing happened so quickly, police were outnumbered".[25]

As an act of vengeance it undoubtedly had public support. As the students danced around the flames singing, "I don't suppose they'll do it again for months and months and months!" onlookers applauded. Crowds flocked to view the wrecked shop, and many of them carried off souvenirs. In the following days messages of congratulation poured in; some from other universities, including Birmingham and Southampton. The Society of Merchant Venturers, an organisation of prominent businessmen and (since 2003) women which supports commercial and charitable initiatives in Bristol, offered the students the use of their sports grounds while they were without their own Sports Pavilion. The Lord Mayor privately expressed his pleasure in the students' action.[26]

The local press, characterising the incident as an amusing rag, was fulsome in its praise – an "exciting scene…wonderfully organised," said the *Bristol Times and Mirror* (*BTM*) on 24 October 1913. The bonfire "made an effective spectacle in the failing light" remarked the *Western Daily Press* on 25 October. In a letter to the *BTM* on 29 October, "Two Undergraduates" suggested that they had performed a public service: "An attack upon a nest of suffragettes is a phase of pest extermination." On 3 November the *BTM* published a poem by a "Bristol undergrad": "But we'll be even with them yet/Lest they forget, lest they forget…" In the December 1913 issue of the university magazine, *Nonesuch*, satirical articles lampooned the suffragettes, and the students' attack was celebrated in verse and drawings. The University authorities let the riot and the celebration of it pass without comment.

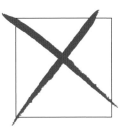

Opposite Page

Police view the damage to the WSPU shop in Queen's Road after two days of rioting by Bristol students, during which one arrest was made. Meanwhile, hundreds of women went to prison after demonstrations in London and elsewhere.

Next page

"A is for Arson, one raw, foggy night…"
The Bristol students celebrate their attack on the WSPU shop in the December 1913 edition of *Nonesuch*.

A is for Arson, one raw, foggy night,

B is the Bonfire, which blazed up so bright.

C is the Chanc'llor we all met last year,

D that Degree-day, which brought him down here.

E for Exams., bringing tearing of hair,

F is the Fresher, so naïve and fair.

G is the Gown, very seldom put on,

H is for Hockey, when summer is gone.

I is the Ink, richly seasoned with slime,

J the Joke, heard for the $(n+1)$th time.

K is the Knowledge, we *hope* to acquire,

L is the Lab. with its odours so dire.

ALPHABET.

M is for Maths. which soften the brain.

N for Nostalgia—sweet home again!

O's One o'clock, when the room quickly clears,

P's for Pavilion, a sight for salt tears.

Q is the Quad. with loud yells forsaken,

R the Revenge, so speedily taken.

S is for Science, and Socials, and Sports,

T is the Tennis, on Combe Dingle courts.

U's University, not yet grown grey,

V's the Vice-Chancellor, mild be his sway!

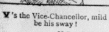

W's for Work, and much Wisdom imbibed,

X is unknown, so it can't be described.

N.B.—Owing to brain-fag, the writer was unable to cope with **Y** and **Z**.

Opposite Page Top

Begbrook mansion,

destroyed by suffragettes

in November 1913.

Opposite Page Bottom

"Birrell's speeches

have cost £3,000.

Release Rachel Pease."

Eastville Park boathouse,

November 1913.

The students' hopes were not realised: the women did it again. On 11 November 1913 Begbrook Mansion in Frenchay was destroyed by fire: £3,000 worth of damage was caused to the twenty-room house. Suffragette literature was found nearby with the note: "Birrell is coming. Rachel Pease is still being tortured". When Birrell duly arrived in Bristol on 13 November there were chemical attacks on a number of postboxes in the city. The next day his North Bristol meeting about Ireland was interrupted when a man threw a dead kitten at him and said, "Torture that instead of women". During Birrell's stay the municipal boathouse at Eastville Park and the boats and canoes it contained were destroyed. On a suffrage newspaper found at the scene was the note: "Birrell's speeches have cost £3,000. Release Rachel Pease".

Mrs Pankhurst had been in America since October 1913. When she arrived in Plymouth on 4 December she was rearrested. She was released after a hunger strike and arrested again in Dover. The militant response was the destruction of a timber yard at Devonport, near Plymouth, on 15 December. The women left a message: "Our reply to the torture of Mrs Pankhurst, and her cowardly arrest at Plymouth". In Bristol on 12 December an unoccupied house only a mile from the University Sports Pavilion, Severn Leigh House in Stoke Road, was "practically gutted" according to *The Times* on 16 December 1913. That month too, a large house in Lansdown, near Bath, was burned down.

The Ruins of Begbrook Frenchay.

GL 102

Joxton 1914

Bristol. Boat House Burnt by Suffragettes at Eastville Park.

The Woman-Torturing Coalition Government

Militancy continued into the New Year, both nationally and locally. Railway stations, piers, hotels, castles, libraries and schools burned, and artefacts and works of art in the British Museum, Royal Academy and other galleries and museums were damaged. On 10 March 1914, the day after Mrs Pankhurst's arrest in Glasgow, Mary Richardson – who had accosted the King in Park Street in 1913 – slashed Diego Velázquez's (1599–1660) painting *The Toilet of Venus*, known as The Rokeby Venus, which had just been purchased by the National Gallery for £45,000.

In Bristol, Imperial Tobacco's timber yard at Ashton Gate burned on 14 March 1914 and the clubhouse at Failand golf links in April. On 26 June an arson attempt was made on an empty house in Bath. The message left at the scene read: "For damages apply to the Woman-Torturing Coalition Government". In July haystacks in Inglesbatch, near Bath, were fired, and a similar message was left: "For damages apply to the Liberal Satanic Government".

There were demonstrations in Bristol restaurants and cinemas. A woman addressed the audience in the Coliseum Picture House (Number 11, Walk) about the torture of political prisoners. She and her companions were thrown out. On 19 February 1914 a woman spoke on the same subject in Lyon's Café in Colston Street, and was herself heckled. On 5 March at the Fortt & Son Tea Rooms in Queen's Road, Clifton, a woman called for customers to protest against forcible feeding.

In early 1914 Bristol opened its International Exhibition at Bower Ashton. It boasted pavilions illustrated with scenes from around the Empire. These included an Indian bazaar, Australian vinery and Malayan rubber plantation. A concert and theatre hall were constructed, and there were fireworks displays and a pageant of Bristol's history. When the Lord Mayor opened the Exhibition on 28 May he was interrupted by a suffragette crying, "They are torturing women in prison." Amidst boos and hisses, she was ejected. (The Exhibition, which had cost £100,000, folded after ten days when the promoters ran into financial difficulties.)

Meanwhile, the Bristol WSPU continued with its usual

fund-raising and campaigning activities, holding outdoor meetings on Durdham Down, Eastville Park, and Bristol Bridge; garden parties, jumble sales and at-homes, selling newspapers, and introducing Saturday afternoon teas at the shop.

As militancy continued, so did government repression. Prison treatment of suffragettes grew more brutal, with the use of drugs on prisoners (which the Government denied) and injuries caused during forcible feeding such as the pouring of food into the lungs or striking of prisoners. Women would not co-operate with the courts. They refused to walk into court and had to be carried to the dock, from where they talked throughout their trials while supporters in the public galleries threw flour and leaflets – and sometimes even hammers. The Government made further attempts to suppress *The Suffragette*, threatening newspaper wholesalers who stocked it. Halls were told not to take bookings from the WSPU. The Government also considered taking action against WSPU subscribers.

Bristol's Churches

By the end of 1913 the WSPU had begun targeting the Church, which they thought should speak out against the torture of forcible feeding. Services had already been interrupted in Westminster Abbey and other places of worship, including Bath Abbey on 26 October, by women praying for suffragette prisoners. At St Paul's, Clifton suffragettes chanted prayers during an evening service in February 1914. On 15 March, prayers for Mrs Pankhurst and Mary Richardson interrupted evensong in All Saints in Clifton. On the same day suffragettes prayed aloud for Mrs Pankhurst in Bristol Cathedral during a sermon preached by a Canadian missionary. The preacher spoke to them afterwards, apparently sympathetically, and accepted a copy of Christabel Pankhurst's book on sexual politics, *The Great Scourge and How to End It.*

In the same month suffragettes were ejected from Holy Trinity, St Philip's; Stoke Bishop Church; St Michael and All Angels, Bishopston; and a service at Christ Church was interrupted, as was a service at St Nicholas Church in June. In July in St Matthew's, Kingsdown, a suffragette stood up and prayed "for the church, which is sanctioning this torture by silence, and denies Christ".[27] She and her friend were pushed out by members of the congregation. That month too a service was interrupted, but there were no ejections, at Emmanuel Church, Clifton (since demolished).

Many churches across the country were targeted by arson, some with explosives. An attempt to burn the Clevedon Parish Church of St Andrew's was made on 21 March 1914 when a fire was lit in the vestry, destroying a number of cassocks and surplices. Suffrage literature was found tied to tombstones. The church is the burial place of Arthur Henry Hallam (1811-1833), whose death was the inspiration for Alfred Lord Tennyson's poem, *In Memoriam.*

On 23 May Annie Kenney went to Lambeth Palace to ask the Archbishop of Canterbury to condemn the treatment of militants and was arrested there under the Cat and Mouse Act after speaking with him. She went back on 28 May after her hunger strike in Holloway and was again arrested. Deputations were also sent to the Bishops of Leicester, Durham, and Bristol.

The deputation to the Bishop of Bristol, the Right Reverend George Forrest Browne, DD (1833–1930), was on 9 March 1914. Bristol organiser Gladys Hazel led the women. She read a statement by Mary Richardson about her experience of forcible feeding. The Bishop, who had long supported access to higher education for women (though he thought they should pursue separate studies from male students at university and should not be awarded degrees), wanted to discuss broader issues of women's suffrage. Miss Hazel stuck to the subject of forcible feeding and asked the Bishop to speak out against it. The Bishop said that he supported the female franchise but he could not condone militancy; women themselves were to blame for forcible feeding because they forced the authorities to do it.

At the end of the interview the women told him they were not satisfied. He retorted that he did not expect that they would be. Suffragettes later demonstrated their dissatisfaction by interrupting a Church Missionary Society meeting which the Bishop was attending on 16 March in the Colston Hall. A woman appealed to him to denounce forcible feeding. She was gagged and dragged outside.

Deputation to the King

On 21 May 1914 Mrs Pankhurst led the WSPU's last great militant raid: a deputation to the King at Buckingham Palace. His Majesty had already refused her request for an audience. The violence meted out to the demonstrators was equal to, if not worse than, that of Black Friday. There were mounted police charges and brutality from the crowd and police, against which some women had tried to arm themselves with whips or clubs.

Sixty-six women and two men were arrested, among them Grace and Aethel Tollemache. Grace was released, but Aethel went on a six-day hunger and thirst strike. During the WSPU prisoners' appearance at Bow Street the next day, there were disturbances in the court room, pictures were slashed at the National Gallery, a mummy case was broken at the British Museum, and a portrait of the King in the Royal Scottish Academy was damaged. Mrs Pankhurst was arrested and released after a five-day hunger and thirst strike in Holloway.

A few days after the deputation, on 27 May, Grace Tollemache and another woman were arrested for breaking windows at Buckingham Palace. They were released without being charged. Further unsuccessful attempts were made to petition the King. There were demonstrations against him in theatres (during one performance a woman shouted "You are a Tsar" at him) and women chained themselves to the railings of Buckingham Palace.

In July 1914 Mrs Pankhurst went to Brittany to recuperate from her imprisonments and hunger strikes, and there she met Christabel. On 24 July *The Times* published her letter to the King warning that the WSPU intended to make another attempt to petition him. Clearly the suffragettes were not ready to give in, but nor was the Government ready to give women the vote. They seemed locked in a war with no prospect of resolution. No one could guess what the end would be, no matter how often the WSPU claimed imminent victory. Yet the Women's Revolution did come to a stop, and a sudden one, when on 4 August Britain declared war on Germany.

Suffragettes and Pacifists

On 10 August 1914 all the suffrage prisoners were unconditionally released. Mrs Pankhurst suspended WSPU activities. The NUWSS dropped all suffrage work and turned itself into a Women's Active Service Corps, while a breakaway NUWSS group formed the Women's International League. The WFL continued its suffrage work, as did Sylvia Pankhurst in the East End.

The war split the women's suffrage movement. Emmeline and Christabel Pankhurst threw themselves behind the war effort, arguing that there was no point fighting for a vote if they had no country to vote in. "As Suffragettes we could not be pacifists at any price," declared Christabel.[28] Other women, like Dorothy Evans, Bristol WSPU organiser in 1913, became pacifists or were at least critical of this particular war.

Christabel Pankhurst returned to England from France and on 8 September 1914 made her first public appearance at the London Opera House, where she spoke about the German Peril. Mrs Pankhurst toured the country making recruitment speeches and handing out white feathers. In October *The Suffragette* was renamed *Britannia*. While other organisations attempted to link women's war work with equal pay and the vote, Emmeline and Christabel Pankhurst demanded compulsory national service for women. They organised a Right to Serve March on 17 July 1915, financed out of Government funds. The WSPU was renamed the Women's Party, and Annie Kenney was among the WSPU women who continued to support the Pankhursts in their new endeavour. They took no further part in the suffrage campaign; instead they demanded votes for servicemen and promised that they would not raise the women's franchise issue again until after an Allied victory.

The WSPU shop on Bristol's Queen's Road was closed and the city prepared for war. Troops and equipment moved through Avonmouth, the Southmead Workhouse was converted to a war hospital, and the Bristol Aeroplane Company at Filton geared up for the production of fighter planes. Many suffragettes went on to serve as nurses and doctors; take over men's jobs in transport, industry and the services; work in munitions factories; or join the women's volunteer police force and auxiliary military services. The militant suffrage campaign was over.

At Last!

The question of the female franchise was raised again in 1916, when concerns were voiced about the servicemen's vote. Many of the men in the trenches had lost their right to vote because they no longer fulfilled the twelve-month residency qualification. Some of the men who were fighting for their country had never been enfranchised.

As soon as Parliament began to debate further franchise reform, even Asquith recognised that the issue of votes for women could not be ignored. On 14 August 1916 he said, "[women] say...If we are going to bring in a new class of electors, on whatever ground of State Service, they point out – and we cannot possibly deny their claim – that during this War the women of this country have rendered as effective service...as any other class of the community."[29]

As the debate continued there were the usual disagreements among the suffrage societies about terms, especially when an age qualification was introduced (should it be thirty or thirty-five?). Mrs Humphry Ward still led the Anti-Suffrage League in protest against the whole idea of women voting. Adult suffragists still criticised gender-based legislation. Only Mrs Pankhurst and Christabel had changed their views. In their patriotic zeal, they declared that the servicemen's vote must take priority, and accused Asquith of raising the spectre of women's votes to prevent an extension of the male franchise.

How far the Government was influenced by gratitude for women's war work or fear of renewed militancy when it granted a limited franchise to women in the 1918 Representation of the People Act is difficult to determine. What is clear is that the 1918 Act fell far short of the WSPU's original demand for the vote for women on the same terms as it is granted to men. It gave men over twenty-one the vote, but enfranchised only women over thirty who met a minimum property qualification, and women graduates over thirty. Full equality came with the Equal Franchise Act of 2 July 1928, which gave women and men over twenty-one the vote.

Some Bristol Suffragettes

Allen, Mary Sophia (1878–1964)

Mary Allen was born in Roath, Glamorgan, and joined the WSPU in 1909 after hearing Annie Kenney speak. She was imprisoned and forcibly fed three times, the first time after participating in a deputation to the House of Commons in February 1909. She was in Holloway for a month. Set to work mending men's shirts, she embroidered "Votes for Women" on the shirt tails. On her release she worked as an unpaid West of England branch organiser in Newport and Cardiff until on 29 June she was arrested for breaking a Home Office window. She returned to Bristol on 4 September when she and Mrs Dove-Willcox were met at Temple Meads by a procession led by Annie Kenney. On 13 November 1909 she was sentenced to fourteen days in Bristol for breaking windows during Winston Churchill's visit to the city. She became a WSPU organiser in Hastings in 1912 and Edinburgh in 1914, where she organised the delivery of pamphlets into King George's carriage during a Royal visit.

When the First World War broke out she joined the Women Police Volunteers (WPV), but was disappointed when at the end of the war the WPV was dismissed from official service. She spent the rest of her career campaigning for the foundation of a permanent female police force. She kept the WPV going on a voluntary basis and was tried for impersonating a police officer in 1920. She also supported the Nazis; she met Hitler in 1934 and urged him to create a force of Nazi policewomen, and became a member of the British Union of Fascists. She died in a Croydon nursing home on 16 December 1964.

Bland, Violet (1863–1940)

Violet Ann Bland was born in Bayston Hill, Shrewsbury. After working as a kitchen maid at Dudmaston Hall (now owned by the National Trust) she moved to Bristol. Here she ran a domestic science college for ladies before settling in London in 1910. In August 1909 she decorated the garden of her Bristol house for a reception for hunger strikers Lillian Dove-Willcox and Mary Allen on their release from prison.

She was arrested on Black Friday, 18 November 1910, when women protesting about the failure of the Conciliation Bill – which they attributed to the Government's "shuffling and delay" – were treated with remarkable brutality by the police.

Violet Bland joined the March 1912 West End window-smashing campaign. This time she was prosecuted, with Violet Ethel Baldock, for breaking windows worth £10. She was imprisoned for four months and while in Aylesbury Prison, went on hunger strike and was forcibly fed.

Codd, Clara (1876–1971)

Clara Codd was born in Bishops Taunton, Barnstaple, North Devon. When she was twenty-three her father died and the family moved to Geneva, where she became a theosophist. On their return to England they settled in Bath. Clara was a member of the Theosophical Society, the Bath branch of the NUWSS and the Social Democratic Federation when in 1907 a speech of Annie Kenney's inspired her to join the WSPU. She worked with Annie in Bristol and Bath, arranging and speaking at meetings and coming in for her share of rough treatment. In 1908 she became Honorary Secretary of the Bath branch of the WSPU.

On 13 October 1908 she was a participant in the "rush the House of Commons" demonstration. Her task was to enter the House of Commons; how she was to achieve this in spite of the 6,000 policemen in Parliament Square was left to her. She spent the day hiding in Westminster Underground Station and at 8pm walked, apparently unnoticed, through the police cordons and into the building. She was soon arrested and served a month in Holloway. On her release she returned to Bristol, where she was met at Temple Meads Railway Station by a decorated wagonette with the banner: "Through thick and thin we ne'er give in". She was taken to a tea party in Clifton and then to an evening reception, where she was presented with a Boadicea brooch.

She was offered a post as a paid WSPU organiser but rejected it in favour of what was to become the remainder of her life's work: lecturing and writing for the Theosophical Society.

Dove-Willcox, Lillian (1875–1963)

Lillian Dove-Willcox (née Dugdale, later Mrs Buckley) was born in Bedminster, Bristol. She was a widow when she joined the WSPU in 1908. In 1911, when Annie Kenney left Bristol, she took over as Honorary Secretary of the local branch.

Lillian was one of the twelve women arrested for breaking windows during the first official WSPU window-smashing raid on 29 June 1909. For this action she was awarded a WSPU medal. After her release she and Theresa Garnett were accused of assaulting two wardresses and again imprisoned. They were released after a three-day hunger strike.

On 16 February 1912 Lillian heckled Bristol MP Charles Hobhouse at an anti-suffrage meeting in the Colston Hall. On 9 March 1913 she was at St Andrew's Hall in Glasgow when Mrs Pankhurst was arrested. She was arrested again on 11 March 1913 while attempting to petition the King at the opening of Parliament.

When Bristol students attacked the WSPU shop in Bristol Lillian was in prison. She had been arrested on 8 October in Piccadilly for attempting to puncture the tyres of a taxi carrying Annie Kenney to prison. She was sentenced to a £2 fine or twenty days.

During the First World War Lillian joined Sylvia Pankhurst's East London Federation of Suffragettes. She was also a member of the Suffragette Fellowship, founded in 1926 to bring together militant women and commemorate the struggle of the suffragettes.

Evans, Dorothy (1888–1944)

London-born Dorothy Evans joined the WSPU in 1907. She left her PE teaching post at Batley Girls' Grammar School in 1909 after her arrest for breaking windows at the Batley Conservative Club. In court she apologised for this action, saying the women's quarrel was with the Liberal Government, not the Conservatives. Her father paid her fine against her will and she was released.

Between 1910 and 1912 she was the WSPU's organiser in Birmingham. She was arrested on 18 November 1910 during the Black Friday demonstration in London. She spent seven days in prison in May 1911 for refusing to pay her dog licence as part of a "no taxation without representation" campaign. In March 1912 she was arrested for her part in the window-smashing campaign in London. She was forcibly fed in prison and released in July. She then worked for WSPU headquarters, travelling about in disguise, engaging in arson, before being sent to Bristol in 1913.

Dorothy Evans's stay in Bristol was a short one and in September 1913 she was organiser at the newly-established WSPU office in Belfast. She was arrested in Belfast in April 1914 and charged with possession of explosives. Her protests during the court proceedings included failing to appear at court on 20 April 1914, instead driving several times past the Central Police Station in a gaily-decorated car. She became a pacifist during the First World War, and continued to work for feminist and socialist causes when the hostilities ended.

Garnett, Theresa (1888–1966)

Leeds-born Theresa Garnett trained as a teacher and joined the WSPU in 1907. In April 1909 she and four other women chained themselves to a statue in the Houses of Parliament, and on 25 June she gatecrashed a reception at the Foreign Office held to celebrate King Edward's birthday. She was not arrested on either of these occasions, but after throwing stones at Government office windows during the 29 June 1909 deputation to the House of Commons she was sentenced to a month's imprisonment.

In Holloway she went on hunger strike and refused to obey the orders of the prison officers. After a scuffle with wardresses she was accused of injuring two of them by biting and kicking. She was rearrested shortly after her release and tried on two counts of assault. One case was dismissed, but on the other she was sentenced to a month in prison. She was released on 8 August after another hunger strike.

In Liverpool in August 1909, under the name Annie O'Sullivan, she was one of the protesters who climbed onto the roofs of houses next to Sun Hall, where the Liberals were holding a meeting. From there they hurled slates onto the hall's roof. In

Walton Gaol she again went on hunger strike, and was released on 26 August.

One of her most notorious actions took place in Bristol when, on 13 November 1909, she assaulted Winston Churchill at Temple Meads Railway Station. She spent a month in Horfield where she went on hunger strike, was forcibly fed, set fire to her cell, and was put in solitary confinement.

Theresa Garnett later said that she had not touched Churchill, and a contemporary report in *The Times* on 15 November did note that she "failed to hit him with the whip. Her hand alone struck him in the face". Mary Blathwayt did not think Churchill had been injured, and noted in her diary that "he seems to have been the most violent".[30]

In 1910 Theresa Garnett was the WSPU organiser at Camberwell, but by now she had had enough of suffragette militancy and left the WSPU. During the First World War she served as a nurse at the Front. After the war she joined the Suffragette Fellowship – founded in 1926 to bring former suffragettes together – and the Women's Freedom League. She was also a member of the Six Point Group, founded in 1921 by Margaret Haig to work for women's equality.

Hazel, Gladys (1881–?)

Gladys Mary Hazel became the organiser for Bristol in 1914 after working as an organiser in Birmingham and Leicester. She was arrested in Birmingham on 24 November 1909, when the WSPU held a meeting in Victoria Square in defiance of an order of the Chief Constable prohibiting meetings there. She was charged with disorderly conduct and obstruction; four other women and two men were also arrested.

She was sentenced to four months' imprisonment for her part in the West End window-smashing raid in March 1912. After her release she went to Dublin and on 28 September was arrested in Grafton Street for distributing handbills advertising a suffrage meeting. The case was dismissed with a caution because there had been no actual obstruction at the time.

On 4 May 1913 she was one of the speakers at a meeting in Manchester protesting against government attacks on the right of free speech following raids and arrests at WSPU headquarters. On 5 December she joined a demonstration outside Exeter jail, where Mrs Pankhurst was on hunger strike. When the prison doctor left the prison, she jumped onto the running board of his car.

She looked after the restocking of the Bristol WSPU shop after Bristol University students wrecked it in October 1913, collecting donations of furniture and books to replace those that had been destroyed. She also led a deputation to the Bishop of Bristol, the Right Reverend George Forrest Browne, DD, on 9 March 1914, to protest against the Church's failure to condemn forcible feeding.

Howey, Elsie (1844–1963)

Elsie Howey was born in Nottinghamshire. After her father's death the family moved to Malvern, Worcestershire, where she lived for the rest of her life. She joined the WSPU in 1907 with her mother Gertrude and elder sister Marie. She was one of the women who hid inside a delivery van and attempted to enter the House of Commons in February 1908. She was arrested again on 30 June when she participated in a deputation to the House. In January 1910 she was arrested with Lady Constance Lytton in Liverpool, and again in March 1912 when she broke windows at Liberty department store in Regent Street during the West End window-smashing campaign.

In December 1912 she was in prison after setting off a fire alarm in Kensington. She had been forcibly fed during earlier imprisonments – she was awarded a WSPU medal in 1910 – but now the injuries she suffered in Holloway were to permanently damage her health. Her throat was so badly injured that her voice was ruined. However, in answer to questions in the House of Commons about her treatment, Home Secretary McKenna insisted that her health was good.

She was a well-known speaker for the WSPU at both small and large gatherings, including the Hyde Park demonstration on

21 June 1908. She also helped with by-election campaigns. She rode dressed as Joan of Arc on a number of occasions, one of which was the funeral of Emily Wilding Davison in June 1913.

During 1909 she was organiser for Plymouth and Torquay and played an active part in West Country militancy. With Vera Wentworth, she harangued Liberal MP Augustine Birrell in March 1909 at Bristol Temple Meads Railway Station. On 1 May she and Vera Holme hid in the organ in the Colston Hall to interrupt Birrell's speech. On 30 July she, Vera Wentworth and Mary Philips were arrested for demonstrating at Lord Carrington's meeting in Exeter and sentenced to a week in prison. On 5 September she, Vera Wentworth and Jessie Kenney assaulted Prime Minister Asquith in Kent, an event which led to the withdrawal from the WSPU of West Country supporters Colonel and Mrs Blathwayt of Batheaston.

In 1923 Elsie Howey became a theosophist. She died in Malvern in 1963.

Lamb, Aeta (1886–1928)

When Annie Kenney came to Bristol in 1907 to start the Bristol and West of England branch of the WSPU, Aeta Lamb, who worked at WSPU headquarters in Clement's Inn, came to help her. Aeta Lamb was born in British Guiana but the family moved to England after her father's death. Her education was patchy: she spent only a year and a half at Notting Hill High School, and subsequently tried working as a teacher but it did not suit her.

She was the first suffragette to visit WSPU sympathisers Colonel, Mrs and Miss Mary Blathwayt in Batheaston, and in 1912 one of the last to plant a tree in their suffragette arboretum. Like the Blathwayts, she had misgivings about escalating militancy, but continued to support the WSPU and was working at WSPU headquarters when the First World War broke out.

Lenton, Lillian (1891–1972)

Lillian Lenton was born in Leicester and trained as a teacher. Her first militant act was taking part in the March 1912 West End window-smashing campaign, for which she was sentenced to two months in prison. She was living in Fishponds, Bristol, by the time she carried out one of the most well-known of the suffragette arson attacks: burning the tea house in Kew Gardens.

With Olive Wharry (who gave her name as Joyce Locke) she was arrested while carrying incendiary material just outside Kew Gardens as the tea house burned on 20 February 1913. While on remand she went on hunger strike, and on 23 February was forcibly fed once. She was released a few hours later suffering from pleurisy caused, apparently, by food entering her lungs. She did not appear for her trial and Olive Wharry, who had also been forcibly fed, faced the charges alone. While the police searched for Lillian, the Home Secretary Reginald McKenna faced tough questions in the House of Commons about the forcible feeding. He was criticised on the one hand for not being able to enforce the law against the suffragettes, and on the other for the cruel practice of forcible feeding.

Lillian evaded the police and, by her own account, continued to commit arson at the rate of two fires a week. On 9 June 1913 she gave herself up in Doncaster for an attempted arson attack for which another woman, who had been mistaken for her, was on trial. She was released from Armley Prison, Leeds, on 17 June after another hunger strike, and gave the police the slip until 7 October, when she was arrested in Paddington Station. She was released from Holloway on 15 October after a hunger strike while on remand, and once again outwitted the police until 22 December, when she was arrested for burning a house in Cheltenham. She was released on Christmas Day after a hunger and thirst strike and was then at large until 4 May 1914, when she was arrested in Birkenhead on the Doncaster charge. Her trial in Leeds on 9 May was interrupted by supporters who protested as she was sentenced to twelve months' imprisonment. She was out again on 12 May after another hunger strike, and was still free when the First World War broke out.

She made so many bold escapes from the police that she was known as "the Pimpernel". Once she left a house surrounded by detectives by disguising herself as a delivery boy. On another occasion she walked past a policeman into Scarborough Railway Station dressed as a nurse and carrying the child of another WSPU member. Another escape was managed when forty or fifty women rushed out of a house and scattered, giving her the opportunity to get away from the detectives outside in the confusion.

During the First World War she served in Serbia with the Scottish Women's Hospital Unit, then worked for the British Embassy, the Save the Children Fund, the Women's Freedom League, and the National Union of Women Teachers. She was Honorary Secretary of the Suffragette Fellowship and unveiled a Fellowship memorial to the suffragettes near Caxton Hall in 1970.

Lidiard, Victoria (1889–1992)

Victoria Lidiard was born Victoria Simmons in Clifton, one of twelve children. The family were vegetarian and she remained interested in animal rights all her life. She learned about inequality early on, when her brothers were given a better education than Victoria and her sisters. She left school at the age of fourteen, learned shorthand at evening classes, and got a job in a photographic studio in Clifton.

With her mother and sisters, she joined the WSPU in 1907 after hearing Annie Kenney speak at a meeting in Clifton. She worked hard in Bristol, chalking pavements, selling *Votes for Women*, and chairing open-air meetings, often enduring insults from men in the audience.

She took part in the West End window-smashing campaign on 4 March 1912, and after her arrest was escorted by a number of policemen to Bow Street. She still had seven stones in her pocket which she tried to lose on the way. To her surprise, when they got to Bow Street the policeman who had walked behind her produced them: he had picked them up as she dropped them. She was sentenced to two months' hard labour, and served six weeks. At her mother's request, Victoria Lidiard did not go on hunger strike. When she returned to Bristol it was to face a summons for defacing a pavement by chalking on it.

When militancy was suspended in 1914, Victoria moved to London, where she ran a guest house and worked in a munitions factory in Battersea. In 1918 she married Major Alexander Lidiard MC, who had been a member of the Men's Political Union for Women's Enfranchisement. After the war the couple trained as opticians and ran practices in Maidenhead and High Wycombe.

Victoria Lidiard joined the campaign for the ordination of women priests and continued to campaign for animal rights. She was grieved when her WSPU prison medal was stolen in a burglary. The last surviving suffragette, she died in Hove at the age of one hundred and two.

Pethick-Lawrence, Emmeline (1867–1954)

Emmeline Pethick-Lawrence was WSPU Treasurer and one of its leaders from 1906 until 1912. She spent part of her childhood in Apsley Road, Clifton, a few doors from her maternal grandmother. When she was eight she attended Greystone House, a boarding school in Devizes, for two years. The family later moved to Weston-super-Mare.

In 1890 Emmeline left the comfortable family home to work in a number of London projects intended to benefit working class girls. There she became involved in socialism. It was the Labour Party MP Keir Hardie who introduced her to Mrs Pankhurst and the WSPU.

Although men could not be members of the WSPU, Emmeline Pethick-Lawrence's husband Frederick (1871–1961) was supportive of her and the Union, and made many contributions to the cause. With Frederick (who was a wealthy newspaper owner) she established, edited and financed the suffragette newspaper *Votes for Women*. She introduced the colours – purple, white and green – in 1908. She was an imaginative fund-raiser with initiatives such as Self-Denial Week, also introduced in 1908. She endured six imprisonments, the first of which in October 1906 caused her a nervous breakdown and forced her early release from prison. She was forcibly fed once, in 1912.

The Pethick-Lawrences parted company with the WSPU in

1912, a rift which was publicly accounted for by a disagreement over the policy of intensified militancy. Despite the painful break with her former friends and colleagues, Emmeline Pethick-Lawrence remained devoted to women's suffrage. In July 1913 she was arrested during a deputation to the House of Commons protesting about the Cat and Mouse Act.

The Pethick-Lawrences were founder members of the United Suffragists in 1914, an attempt to unite militant and non-militants, and gave *Votes for Women* to the new organisation. Emmeline remained friendly with Sylvia Pankhurst, to whom she gave financial support. She was Treasurer of the Women's International League for Peace and Freedom from 1915 to 1922, stood as a Labour Parliamentary candidate in 1918, and was President of the Women's Freedom League from 1926 to 1935.

Richardson, Mary (1882/3–1961)

Mary Richardson was brought up in Canada, although she may have been born in Britain, where she settled when she was sixteen. She was a freelance journalist when she joined the WSPU in 1909, and worked in Kilburn WSPU, then in the WSPU shop on Charing Cross Road. She knew Bristol organiser Lillian Dove-Willcox, and stayed with her at her cottage near Tintern Abbey to recover from one of her hunger strikes. On 11 March 1913 she was arrested for breaking windows at the Home Office in protest at the arrest of Dove-Willcox and others for attempting to present a petition to the King at the opening of Parliament. She was sentenced to one month in prison.

On 4 July 1913 she attempted to present a petition to the King during his visit to Bristol. It was the arrest of Mary Richardson and Rachel Pease for arson which prompted the destruction of the Bristol University Sports Pavilion on 23 October 1913. She was released on 25 October with suspected appendicitis after being forcibly fed.

She was arrested again on 10 March 1914 for damaging *The Toilet of Venus*, known as The Rokeby Venus, a painting by Diego Velázquez in the National Gallery, in protest at the arrest of Mrs Pankhurst. For this she was sentenced to six months in prison. Her doctor suspected she had been given bromide while incarcerated, and the prison authorities retaliated by accusing her of smuggling in tablets which had induced vomiting. At the end of July she was operated on for appendicitis. Her final arrest was on 27 August 1914 for taking part in a deputation to the Home Office to demand the release of all suffragette prisoners. The Government had already announced an amnesty and the deputation was released without charge.

Mary Richardson resumed her writing, publishing a novel, poetry collections and an autobiography. She joined both the United Suffragists and the Suffragettes of the WSPU, an organisation of former WSPU members who continued the campaign for the vote. She later joined the Labour Party, and stood as a parliamentary candidate four times. However, between 1932 and 1935 she was a member of Oswald Mosley's New Party and then the British Union of Fascists.

Walters, Alice Mary (c.1859–?)

In 1913 Alice Walters, a teacher, was Honorary Secretary of the Bristol branch of the WSPU. She was imprisoned for a week in March that year for refusing to pay her dog licence. On 27 June she smashed a window in Regent Street Post Office with a hammer. The attack was one of a number of simultaneous raids made on post offices throughout the country. On 10 July she was sentenced at Bow Street Magistrates Court to four months' imprisonment.

In Holloway Alice and others petitioned the Home Office for political prisoner status and when this was refused they went on hunger strike. After two days she was forcibly fed. The procedure affected her so badly she feared that if a second attempt was made she would lose her sanity. In fact, she was so distressed that she was released and brought back to Bristol by two wardresses.

Alice was one of the two women who were in the WSPU shop on Queen's Road when it was wrecked by students from the University of Bristol on 24 October 1913.

She also had an interest in the theatre and took the part of Maudie Spark in the 1910 performance of Cicely Hamilton's *How the Vote Was Won* at Bristol's Prince's Theatre. On 15 March 1913 a "Miss Walters" – who may have been Alice – performed in Evelyn Glover's suffrage play *A Chat With Mrs Chicky* at the Co-operative Hall in Fishponds.

Wentworth, Vera (1890–1957)

Vera Wentworth (born Jessie Spinks) was a London shop assistant and trade unionist. She and Elsie Howey were among the women imprisoned for attempting to approach the House of Commons in a delivery van in 1908. She was kept in prison for an extra day for carving "Votes for Women" on her cell wall. She told the Governor of Holloway that one day the prison would fall into disuse and become a tourist attraction, "and visitors will be shown the inscription, and women, then with the glory of the vote, will shudder and thank providence that they did not live in these days."[31]

Vera Wentworth and Elsie Howey went on to be arrested on a number of other occasions: during the demonstration of 30 June 1908; in March 1909 when they accosted Liberal MP Augustine Birrell at Temple Meads Railway Station; and in July 1909 in Exeter with Mary Phillips for demonstrating against Lord Carrington in July 1909.

Vera also joined Elsie and Jessie Kenney in more violent actions. In 1909 the three turned up in Clovelly, Devon, where Prime Minister Asquith was spending the weekend, and followed him into the church. Asquith fled from a side door. On 5 September 1909 they caught up with him again in Lympne in Kent. This time he did not escape. They struck him, and later threw stones through the window of Lympne Castle when he was at dinner.

Vera Wentworth was arrested in Bristol on 12 November 1909 during disturbances associated with the visit of Winston Churchill to the city, when she broke windows at the Liberal Club. She went on hunger strike in Horfield prison and was forcibly fed.

She took part in demonstrations in London and was arrested

on 18 November 1910 (Black Friday), 21 November 1911 (when in court she blamed Asquith for the damage done by the suffragettes), and March 1912 in the West End window-smashing campaign. While in prison in Holloway her one-act play *An Allegory* was performed by suffrage prisoners. Between 1912 and 1914 she studied history and economy at St Andrew's University. In the Second World War she worked in Air Raid Precautions (ARP).

A Walk with the Bristol Suffragettes

(1) 23 Gordon Road, Clifton

Our walk starts at 23 Gordon Road because it is here that a blue plaque marks the residence of WSPU organiser Annie Kenney. She was sent to the city by Emmeline Pankhurst in 1907 to establish the Bristol and West of England branch of the WSPU. In fact, Annie Kenney lived at several addresses in the city. She was in Neville House on Whiteladies Road until 1909, when she moved to Downe House in Clifton. She lived at 23 Gordon Road in 1910, then at 16 Arlington Villas (Number 3, Walk) before being recalled to London in October 1911. Lancashire-born Kenney was one of the Pankhursts' most loyal followers, and continued to work with them when the WSPU turned into the war-propagandising Women's Party.

 With your back to the house, turn right and walk to the end of the road. Turn right into York Place (enjoying the views over Bristol on your left).

23 Gordon Road, Clifton.

② 5 York Place, Clifton

5 York Place was the Bristol residence of Leeds suffragette Theresa Garnett, who on 13 November 1909 attacked Winston Churchill at Temple Meads Railway Station. Churchill's visit to Bristol was the focus of several days of suffragette activity, including window-smashing and heckling during his speeches at the Colston Hall. A Bristol lawyer later characterised Garnett's treatment in Horfield Prison – where she served one month for the attack, went on hunger strike and ended up in the prison hospital – as "brutal". Although Garnett initially embraced militancy, and was for a time a WSPU organiser in Camberwell, she left the WSPU in late 1910 when militancy escalated.

> Walk to the end of York Place and turn right onto Clifton Road. At the end of Clifton Road turn right onto Queen's Road and continue past the top of Gordon Road and the University of Bristol Students' Union. Cross at the zebra crossing and turn left into Pembroke Road. Cross the road and turn into Arlington Villas, which is first on the right.

③ 16 Arlington Villas

At the time of the 1911 census resistance Annie Kenney was living at 16 Arlington Villas. She spent the night at 9 Whatley Road and refused to fill in her form, except for giving her occupation as "Suffragette".

> Follow the road round to the right. Cross St Paul's Road into Westbourne Place. Walk down and turn left onto Queen's Road to the Victoria Rooms.

4 The Victoria Rooms

The Victoria Rooms, which now house the Music Department of the University of Bristol, opened in 1842. They were designed to replace the Assembly Rooms on Clifton Mall. Originally the forecourt was flanked by two sphinxes, but in 1911 these were removed and the fountain and statue of Edward VII placed here. On 4 July 1913 King George came to Bristol to view the statue of his father. The original hall was destroyed by fire in 1934.

Many famous speakers appeared in the Rooms, including Charles Dickens and Oscar Wilde. Here too appeared the WSPU's most famous women: Mrs Pankhurst, Mrs Pethick-Lawrence, Christabel Pankhurst, Annie Kenney, and many others. The Rooms were also the setting for other campaigns before the WSPU came to Bristol. In September 1869 the National Campaign Against the Contagious Diseases Acts was launched here, and the Bristol and West of England Society for Women's Suffrage held meetings here in the 1870s.

WSPU meetings at the Rooms did not always pass without incident. On 8 November 1907 Mary Blathwayt was in the audience when Annie Kenney and Christabel Pankhurst spoke, and brawling men had to be thrown out. On 3 April 1908 six professional boxers were hired to protect speakers from medical students, who interrupted Mrs Pankhurst's speech.

Continue round the front of the Victoria Rooms and cross Whiteladies Road at the zebra crossing with the Royal West of England Academy in front of you. Turn right in front of the RWA and walk straight on, crossing over another zebra crossing to pass a row of shops. Cross University Road and turn right to cross at the traffic lights. The WSPU shop and office was the second building on the left from the end of the terrace at the entrance to Berkeley Square.

The Victoria Rooms, Bristol.

(5) 37 Queen's Road

The WSPU shop originally opened at 33 Queen's Road in 1908, and moved to Number 37 in April 1909. The shop sold a range of WSPU goods, which might have included cigarettes, chocolate, books, tea, belts, bags, hatpins, scarves, postcards and soap. Posters and photographs were displayed in the window. Mary Blathwayt ran the Bristol shop and later, the Bath shop. The NUWSS opened its own Bristol shop on Whiteladies Road in 1909.

WSPU goods were also sold at other outlets, including fêtes, jumble sales and bazaars. In May 1913 Bristol members were reminded that they were responsible for the Basket, Cushion and Lampshade stall at the Suffragette Summer Festival in London in June: "Let us have scores of all three…each shipshape and Bristol fashion" pleaded the organiser.[32]

The Fortt & Son Tea Rooms were in Queen's Road. It was one of many Bristol restaurants where diners had their meals interrupted by suffragette protests.

Facing the site of the WSPU shop, turn left and walk downhill. On the opposite side of the road are the Bristol City Art Gallery and Museum (opened 1905) and the University of Bristol Wills Memorial Building (opened 1925). Turn right onto Park Street.

 Park Street

Many other suffrage and reform organisations had their headquarters in this street. In the 1880s the Bristol and West of England Society for Women's Suffrage, which affiliated to the NUWSS in 1898, was based at Number 20 (renumbered 69). The premises were also the lodgings of the Secretary, Helen Blackburn (1842–1903).

47 Park Street was the home of Mary Estlin (1820–1902), Secretary of the Bristol and Clifton Ladies Anti-Slavery Society, which was formed in 1840. Many of the anti-slavery campaigners went on to join suffrage organisations. The Women's Total Abstinence Union had its office at Number 33, and the Hannah More Hall commemorated the work of this Fishponds-born bluestocking, anti-slavery campaigner and charity-school founder. Hannah More (1745–1833) taught in her elder sisters' school for young ladies (since demolished) which was on the site now occupied by 43 Park Street. Annie Kenney and Georgina Brackenbury (1865–1949) were among WSPU speakers who appeared at the Hannah More Hall.

It was on Park Street on 4 July 1913 that Mary Richardson attempted to throw a petition into King George's carriage during his visit to the city to see the new statue of Edward VII outside the Victoria Rooms, and attend the Royal Show on Durdham Down. Richardson was a keen militant and achieved particular notoriety when she slashed Velázquez's painting, *The Toilet of Venus* (known as The Rokeby Venus), in the National Gallery in protest at Mrs Pankhurst's treatment. Richardson declared that the WSPU leader was "being slowly murdered by a Government of Iscariot politicians".[33]

Turn into Charlotte Street, first on the right.

(7) 20 Charlotte Street

A blue plaque unveiled in 2004 at 20 Charlotte Street marks the birthplace of Emmeline Pethick-Lawrence (1867–1954), WSPU Treasurer and one of its leaders from 1906 until the split with the Pankhursts in 1912.

Retrace your steps to Park Street, turn right and continue down the hill to College Green.

(8) Bristol Cathedral

In 1914 the WSPU targeted churches throughout the country, interrupting services and in some cases causing damage to buildings. During an evening service in Bristol Cathedral on 14 March a woman prayed out loud for "Mrs Pankhurst and other women persecuted for conscience's sake", and the prayer was followed by a "deep and reverent silence".[34] The preacher, a Canadian missionary, spoke to the woman in the Chapter House and she gave him a copy of Christabel Pankhurst's polemic on sexual relations, *The Great Scourge and How to End It*.

Cross Park Street at the crossing after the Cathedral, turn right, and follow the road (College Green) round to the left into the Centre. Walk along St Augustine's Parade, passing the Hippodrome Theatre. If you look across the Centre from here you will see the top of Baldwin Street, where the windows of the Board of Trade offices were smashed as part of the protests during Winston Churchill's 1909 visit to Bristol. Continue past the theatre and turn left up Colston Street to the Colston Hall.

⑨ The Colston Hall

The Colston Hall was designed as a place for meetings and concerts and built on the site of a Carmelite priory. Colston's School occupied the site between 1707 and 1857, and sold the land to the Colston Hall developers in 1861. The priory was demolished to make way for the Hall. The main Hall opened in 1867, was destroyed by fire in 1898, rebuilt and reopened in 1900. Liberals, the WSPU and other suffrage organisations, and anti-suffragists all held meetings here.

On the afternoon of 1 May 1909 Elsie Howey, who had come to Bristol to work as an unpaid organiser and was staying with Annie Kenney, hid in the organ with Vera Holme in order to interrupt Liberal MP Augustine Birrell's meeting that evening. It was one of the most successful of many suffragette protests at the Colston Hall. The premises had been searched and the building pronounced free of suffragettes before the meeting started. Birrell was in mid-speech when, as if from nowhere, came the cry, "Votes for women!" Being ejected from the Colston Hall was not an amusing experience – women usually ended up bruised and dishevelled after their struggles with stewards and men in the audience.

⑩ Colston Street

Bristolians could not even be sure of having a cup of tea free of suffragettes. At lunchtime on 19 February 1914 diners in Lyon's Café on Colston Street had their meals interrupted when a suffragette stood up and talked about forcible feeding. She and other women were asked to leave and they distributed leaflets as they left.

Continue uphill past the Colston Hall and turn left into Lower Park Row, which joins Park Row. Continue into Park Row, past the Red Lodge on the left. On the opposite side of the road, on the corner of Woodland Road, is what remains of the Coliseum.

⑪ The Coliseum, Park Row

Filmgoers too were pestered by suffragettes. The wedge-shaped Coliseum Picture House was part of a much bigger site that was originally an exhibition hall and skating rink. It was converted to a cinema in 1912. On Saturday 7 February 1914 a suffragette and her companions were thrown out by attendants for trying to distribute leaflets and speak to the audience about the torture of political prisoners.

The Coliseum closed in 1914. It was bombed on 24 November 1940 and only the walls were left standing. It is now owned by the University of Bristol. If you cross the road you can see a memorial to Nipper, the dog who featured on the HMV record company's logo.

The Coliseum. Note the statue of "Nipper" above the door.

(12) Site of Prince's Theatre, Park Row

The Prince's Theatre was opposite the Coliseum and was built by manager James Chute (1808–1878) next door to his own home on Park Row. It opened in 1867 and was destroyed in the air raid on 24 November 1940. The Theatre's existence is now commemorated in the names of the blocks of flats constructed over the site: Irving House and Terry House. Many famous performers, from actors to music hall stars, performed on the Prince's stage, and the theatre became famous for its pantomimes. It was here on 5 November 1910 that the local WSPU organised a performance of Cicely Hamilton's *A Pageant of Great Women.*

 Carry straight on back to Queen's Road (towards the Wills Memorial Building) and pass the the top of Park Street. Turn right to walk back to the site of the WSPU shop.

(13) 37 Queen's Road

The walk ends back at the site of the WSPU shop, which was the scene of spectacular disturbances on 24 and 25 October 1913, when Bristol University students wrecked it in retaliation for the destruction by fire of the University Sports Pavilion at Coombe Dingle during the night of 23 October. On the day of the first attack Alice Walters and a woman who would not give her name were inside. Walters later protested that the local WSPU knew nothing about the attack on the Sports Pavilion. The women had, however, been aware of the planned revenge and had warned the police of impending trouble in the early afternoon. They were promised police protection, which in the event was not forthcoming, and the shop and office were wrecked. Bonfires were lit in the street, goods looted and stink bombs thrown. The police later said it all happened too quickly for them to make any arrests.

After the attack the WSPU was temporarily housed at 16 Berkeley Square, which was later owned by the University of Bristol. Appeals to WSPU members for help and donations soon saw the shop refurbished and it reopened in December.

 To return to the start of the walk follow Queen's Road back round to the top of Gordon Road.

St Paul's Road

Arlington Villas

Whiteladies Road

Pembroke Road

Queen's Road

Queen's Road

Queen's Road

Queen's Road

Gordon Road

Clifton Road

York Place

1	23 Gordon Road	8	Bristol Cathedral
2	5 York Place	9	The Colston Hall
3	16 Arlington Villas	10	Colston Street
4	The Victoria Rooms	11	The Coliseum, Park Row
5	37 Queen's Road	12	Site of Prince's Theatre, Park Row
6	Park Street		
7	20 Charlotte Street	13	37 Queen's Road

N

A Women's Suffrage Timeline

1832	The First Reform Act excludes women from the franchise by granting the vote to any "male person" who meets the property qualification.
7 June 1866	Liberal MP John Stuart Mill presents to Parliament a petition for the female franchise based on the property qualification.
1867	The Second Reform Act increases the male franchise. Further women's petitions support John Stuart Mill's failed attempt to move an amendment to substitute the word "person" for "male person".
1884	The Third Reform Act excludes women from the franchise.
October 1896	Following the 1895 general election, the London, Manchester and other provincial suffrage societies form the National Union of Women's Suffrage Societies (NUWSS).
10 October 1903	Emmeline Pankhurst founds the Women's Social and Political Union in Manchester. The WSPU's aim is to obtain the vote for women on the same terms as men, and its policy is to oppose any government which does not grant women the vote.
20 February 1904	Christabel Pankhurst raises the issue of votes for women during a Free Trade League meeting in Manchester addressed by Liberal MP Winston Churchill. She later described this as the first militant act.
13 October 1905	Christabel Pankhurst and Annie Kenney are arrested at a Liberal meeting in the Free Trade Hall in Manchester. They are the first women to go to prison for the cause.
13 February 1907	The day after Parliament opens, women marching from Caxton Hall (the first Women's Parliament) to the House of Commons with a resolution protesting about the omission of votes for women from the King's speech are brutally treated by the police. Christabel and Sylvia Pankhurst are among the fifty-four women arrested.
October 1907	A split in the WSPU about the Pankhursts' "autocratic" governing style leads to the formation of the Women's Freedom League. The WSPU founds its newspaper, *Votes for Women*. In the same year the Women's Anti-Suffrage League is formed, as well as a Men's League for Opposing Women's Suffrage. These organisations merge in 1910 to form the National League for Opposing Women's Suffrage.
April 1908	Herbert Henry Asquith replaces Henry Campbell-Bannerman as Prime Minister.
13 June 1908	The NUWSS stages a procession of 13,000 women to the Albert Hall.

21 June 1908	The WSPU holds a procession and Hyde Park meeting. The Government continues to refuse to give facilities to a women's suffrage bill.
30 June 1908	Women demonstrating in Parliament Square are treated with such brutality by police and other men that two women retaliate by breaking windows at 10 Downing Street. Mrs Pankhurst endorses their actions. It is the first damage caused by suffragettes.
29 June 1909	The eighth Women's Parliament sees the first official WSPU window-breaking; the windows of several government buildings are broken. One hundred and eight women are arrested and later released, with the exception of stone-throwers, who are sent to Holloway. Here they go on hunger strike, following the example earlier that summer of Marion Wallace Dunlop, the first hunger striker.
January 1910	Prime Minister Asquith calls a general election. Militancy is suspended during the election, but the WSPU campaigns in forty constituencies. After the election an all-party Conciliation Committee is established to draft a franchise bill acceptable to all parties.
6 May 1910	Death of King Edward VII. All WSPU propaganda stops until after the funeral.
14 June 1910	The Conciliation Bill is introduced. The WSPU formally announces a truce and a halt to militancy. Suffrage societies demonstrate in support of the bill. The bill subsequently passes its second reading. However, Asquith refuses to grant further facilities.
18 November 1910	On the day that Parliament reconvenes, the WSPU holds its ninth Women's Parliament. On learning that Asquith has not given facilities to the Conciliation Bill, a deputation is sent to the House of Commons. The brutality that follows is so extreme that this becomes known as Black Friday. Over a hundred women are arrested. Mrs Pankhurst's sister and another woman later die from their injuries. The Government refuses to hold an inquiry into the conduct of the police.
January 1911	Asquith is returned after a general election. The WSPU renews its truce in the hope that the Conciliation Bill will proceed.
5 May 1911	An amended Conciliation Bill is introduced and it passes its second reading. The Government promises that time will be given in the next session for the consideration of the bill. The WSPU is now confident of success.

7 November 1911	Asquith announces that a Government franchise bill capable of amendment to include women will be introduced in the next Parliamentary session. Suffragettes and suffragists believe that the Government is using the Manhood Suffrage Bill to defeat the Conciliation Bill.
21 November 1911	At the tenth Women's Parliament (held during Mrs Pankhurst's absence in America) the WSPU renews militancy with a deputation to the House of Commons and organised window-smashing. Two hundred and twenty women and three men are arrested.
1 and 4 March 1912	On 1 March Mrs Pankhurst heads an unannounced window-smashing raid in Downing Street. She is sentenced to two months' imprisonment. On 4 March one hundred and twenty-one women are arrested after a mass window-smashing raid in the West End and around Whitehall.
5 March 1912	The police raid WSPU headquarters and arrest Mr and Mrs Pethick-Lawrence and Mabel Tuke. Christabel flees to Paris from where she directs the movement and edits the newspaper *Votes for Women*.
28 March 1912	The Conciliation Bill is defeated.
8 April 1912	Mrs Pankhurst's sentence for window-smashing is remitted and she is released on bail. Instead she is to be tried on charges of conspiracy with the Pethick-Lawrences and Mabel Tuke. The trial ends on 22 May with sentences of nine months for the defendants. They go on hunger strike in support of their demand for political prisoner status. They are released in June.
12 July 1912	Christabel Pankhurst institutes a campaign of secret arson attacks.
17 July 1912	The Government introduces its Reform Bill, which makes no provision for votes for women.
October 1912	The Pethick-Lawrences are unhappy about the increasingly militant tactics and are asked to leave the WSPU by Christabel and Mrs Pankhurst. They retain ownership of the magazine *Votes for Women*. The WSPU introduces its own magazine, *The Suffragette*.
18 January 1913	A few days before the 18 January debate on the women's suffrage amendments to the Government Reform Bill, Mrs Pankhurst calls a halt to militancy. On 17 January the Speaker rules that certain Government amendments not connected with women's suffrage would so change the character of the bill that a new one must be introduced. On 18 January Asquith accepts the Speaker's ruling.

27 January 1913	Asquith announces the withdrawal of the Reform Bill. The WSPU truce ends in unprecedented militancy. Telephone wires are cut, works of art destroyed, boathouses and sports pavilions burned, the tea house in Kew Gardens is burned and three orchid glass houses smashed and the plants torn up, empty houses are set on fire, and golf courses vandalised.
18 February 1913	A house under construction for David Lloyd George at Walton-on-the-Hill is destroyed by fire.
24 February 1913	In a meeting in Cardiff Mrs Pankhurst accepts responsibility for militant acts. She is arrested the next day and charged with having "counselled and procured" the people who destroyed Lloyd George's house.
25 March 1913	The Government rushes through The Prisoners (Temporary Discharge for Ill-Health) Act – the Cat and Mouse Act. Under this Act hunger-strikers, if certified to be unfit to remain in prison by prison doctors, are to be released on licence to recover from their hunger strike and then rearrested when they are well enough to continue their sentences. The power to forcibly feed prisoners is retained.
2 April 1913	Mrs Pankhurst is tried and sentenced to three years' penal servitude. She is released on special licence (the Cat and Mouse Act not yet being in operation) after nine days' hunger strike. The pattern of her hunger strikes and releases on licence is to be repeated over the coming months.
15 April 1913	The Home Office bans WSPU open-air meetings.
30 April 1913	The police raid WSPU headquarters and arrest personnel, seize copy prepared for *The Suffragette* and, two days later, arrest the manager of the printing company.
2 May 1913	Annie Kenney and other WSPU staff are put on trial for conspiracy to commit malicious damage. Sentences passed in June range from twelve to eighteen months' imprisonment. The prisoners embark on a cycle of hunger strike and rearrest under the Cat and Mouse Act.
5 May 1913	A Private Members' Suffrage Bill is defeated.
4 June 1913	Emily Wilding Davison is injured when she throws herself under the King's horse during the Derby at Epsom Downs Racecourse. She dies on 8 June 1913.
26 July 1913	The Suffrage Pilgrimage organised by the NUWSS ends with a mass meeting in Hyde Park. The Pilgrimage has been going on for some weeks as people march to London from across the country.

July to December 1913	Mrs Pankhurst, WSPU leaders, and rank and file suffragettes are in and out of prison under the Cat and Mouse Act. Mrs Pankhurst introduces the thirst and sleep strike, and evades arrest when she can. In August she and Annie Kenney join Christabel Pankhurst in Paris, and in October Mrs Pankhurst goes on a fund-raising tour in America. She is rearrested on her return to the UK on 4 December 1913. Meanwhile militancy continues. Mansions are destroyed, pillar boxes attacked, tennis courts and golf courses damaged with acid, "dummy" bombs left on the London Underground and in public buildings, real bombs used in arson attacks, and church services interrupted. One estimate puts the value of damage by arson in 1913 at £510,150. A Cat and Mouse Act Repeal Committee is established. Male suffrage supporters hire meeting places so that women can speak at them. Keir Hardie and others form a Free Speech Defence Committee.
21 May 1914	Mrs Pankhurst leads the last great WSPU militant deputation to the King at Buckingham Palace. Thousands of police are brought in to repel them. Sixty-six women and two men are arrested. Mrs Pankhurst is among the arrested and promptly goes on hunger and thirst strike.
4 August 1914	Britain declares war on Germany.
10 August 1914	All suffragette prisoners are released. Mrs Pankhurst suspends WSPU activities.
16 April 1915	*The Suffragette* reappears after a short break. On 15 October it is relaunched as *Britannia*, a pro-war paper. Christabel has returned to England to campaign against the "German peril" and Mrs Pankhurst is touring the country making recruitment speeches, calling for compulsory service for war work by women, and handing out white feathers.
17 July 1915	The WSPU, calling itself the Women's Party, organises a Right to Serve March, which is paid for from government funds.
5 November 1915	As the demand for the enfranchisement of the men at the Front grows, the Government responds by delaying the general election for eight months. Amidst rumours that a Government Franchise Bill is to be introduced, those suffrage societies that are still active write to Asquith to remind him of the women's claims.
6 February 1918	The Representation of the People Act is passed, granting the Parliamentary vote to men over twenty-one and women over thirty who are occupiers, or wives of occupiers, of land or premises of not less than £5 annual value, and to women university graduates aged over thirty.

1918	Under The Parliament (Qualification of Women) Act, women can now stand for Parliament. Seventeen women do so, including Christabel Pankhurst, who is unsuccessful.
23 December 1919	Under The Sex Disqualification (Removal) Act, women are no longer barred from civil or judicial offices (including judge, barrister and solicitor), from any profession, or from membership of any incorporated society.
2 July 1928	The Equal Franchise Act gives women the vote on the same terms as men: all men and women over the age of twenty-one have the vote.

There is a more detailed Timeline available as a free download at www.lucienneboyce.com.

Note on Sources and Further Reading

There are a huge number of books about both the militant and non-militant suffrage campaigns. For this account I have used published autobiographies, diaries, newspaper and magazine accounts, and a number of archives including those held at the Women's Library in London, the Museum of London, Bristol Central Reference Library, and the London Library. All sources have to be approached with caution: memories fade, writers are biased to one viewpoint or another, journalists get details wrong. The selective booklist below is not exhaustive, but if you want to find out more about the campaign for the women's vote it might help you get started.

Newspapers and Journals

Britannia
Bristol Evening Post
Bristol Times and Mirror
The Guardian
The Suffragette
The Times
Votes for Women
Western Daily Press

Biographies and Autobiographies

David, Edward, ed., *Inside Asquith's Cabinet: From the Diaries of Charles Hobhouse* (London: Murray, 1977)

Davis, Mary, *Sylvia Pankhurst: A Life in Radical Politics* (Sterling, VA: Pluto Press, 1999)

Hamilton, Cicely, *Life Errant* (London: Dent, 1935)

Jenkins, Roy, *Asquith: Portrait of a Man and an Era* (New York: Chilmark Press, 1964)

Kenney, Annie, *Memories of a Militant* (London: Edward Arnold & Co, 1924)

Lytton, Constance, *Prisons and Prisoners: The Stirring Testimony of a Suffragette* (London: Virago, 1988)

Owen, Roger, *Lord Cromer: Victorian Imperialist, Edwardian Proconsul* (Oxford: Oxford University Press, 2004)

Pankhurst, Christabel, *Unshackled: The Story of How We Won the Vote* (London: Hutchinson, 1959)

Pankhurst, E. Sylvia, *The Suffragette Movement: An Intimate Account of Persons and Ideals* (London: Virago, 1977)

Pankhurst, Emmeline, *My Own Story: The Autobiography of Emmeline Pankhurst* (London: Virago, 1979)

Pethick-Lawrence, Emmeline, *My Part in a Changing World* (London: Victor Gollanz, 1938)

Roberts, Katherine, *Pages From the Diary of a Militant Suffragette* (Letchworth and London: Garden City Press, 1911)

Romero, Patricia W., *E. Sylvia Pankhurst: Portrait of a Radical* (New Haven and London: Yale University Press, 1987)

Reference Books

Crawford, Elizabeth, *The Women's Suffrage Movement: A Reference Guide 1866–1928* (London: Routledge, 2001)

Local History

Boyce, Lucienne, 'A is for Arson', *Nonesuch*, (Spring 2003), pp. 19–21

Brierley, Lorna and Helen Reid, *Go Home and Do the Washing! Three Centuries of Pioneering Bristol Women* (Bristol: Broadcast Books, 2000)

Carleton, Don, *The Prince's of Park Row* (Bristol: Bristol Branch of the Historical Association, 1983)

Carleton, Don, *A University for Bristol* (Bristol: University of Bristol Press, 1984)

Dobbie, B.M. Willmott, *A Nest of Suffragettes in Somerset* (The Batheaston Society, 1979)

Hammond, Cynthia and Dan Brown, *Suffragettes in Bath: Activism in an Edwardian Arboretum* (Bath: Bath in Time, 2011)

Malos, Ellen, 'Bristol Women in Action, 1839-1919: The right to vote and the need to earn a living' in *Bristol's Other History*, ed. by Ian Bild (Bristol: Bristol Broadsides, 1983), pp. 97–128

Stephenson, Dave, *Bristol Cinemas* (Stroud: Tempus Publishing, 2005)

Tanner, S.J., *How the Women's Suffrage Movement Began in Bristol Fifty Years Ago* (Bristol: Carlyle Press, 1918)

Whittingham, Sarah, *The University of Bristol: A History* (Bristol: University of Bristol Press, 2009)

Suffrage Histories

Abrams, Fran, *Freedom's Cause: Lives of the Suffragettes* (London: Profile Books, 2003)

Cowman, Krista, *Women of the Right Spirit: Paid Organisers of the Women's Social and Political Union (WSPU) 1904–18*, Gender in History series (Manchester: Manchester University Press, 2007)

Holton, Sandra Stanley, *Suffrage Days: Stories from the Women's Suffrage Movement* (London: Routledge, 1996)

Jounou, Maroula and June Purvis, eds., *The Women's Suffrage Movement: New Feminist Perspectives* (Manchester and New York: Manchester University Press, 1998)

Liddington, Jill, *One Hand Tied Behind Us: A History of the Women's Suffrage Movement* (London: Virago, 1978)

Marlow, Joyce, *Votes for Women: the Virago Book of Suffragettes* (London: Virago, 2000)

McPhee, Carol and Ann Fitzgerald, eds, *The Non-Violent Militant: Selected Writings of Teresa Billington-Greig,* Women's Source Library (London: Routledge & Kegan Paul, 1987)

Purvis, June and Sandra Stanley Holton, eds, *Votes for Women* (London: Routledge, 2000)

Raeburn, Antonia, *Militant Suffragettes* (Newton Abbot: Victorian (& Modern History) Book Club, 1974; first published by Michael Joseph,1973)

Strachey, Ray, *The Cause: A Short History of the Women's Movement in Great Britain* (London: Virago, 1978)

Watson, Norman, *Suffragettes and the Post* (Robertson Printers, Forfar, Angus, 2010)

Suffrage Imagery

Atkinson, Diane, *The Suffragettes in Pictures*, Museum of London (Stroud: Sutton Publishing, 1996)

Atkinson, Diane, *The Purple White and Green: Suffragettes in London 1906–14* (London: Museum of London, 1992)

Atkinson, Diane, *Funny Girls: Cartooning for Equality* (London: Penguin Books, 1997)

Tickner, Lisa, *The Spectacle of Women: Imagery of the Suffrage Campaign 1907–14* (Chicago: University of Chicago Press, 1988)

Acknowledgements and Picture Credits

I am very grateful to the people who have helped me with this book. My thanks go to the friendly and helpful staff at the Bristol Record Office; to the librarians at Bristol Central Library and Dawn Dyer in particular; to the staff at the University of Bristol Library, the London Library and the Museum of London. I'd also like to thank Michael Freeman for taking the photographs for the walk, and Joe Mordle of Pinecone Design for the map. Many thanks to my sister and editor, Glynis van Uden, and author Sarah Whittingham for reading and commenting on the text. A big thank you to Helen Hart and the team at SilverWood Books.

Picture Credits

1. Mrs Emmeline Pankhurst – Museum of London, c.1909 (Image 006046)
2. Suffragette March in Hyde Park – Museum of London, 1910 (Image 005644)
3. Annie Kenney – Museum of London, c.1910 (Image 002080)
4. Self-Denial Week – Museum of London, c.1910 (Image 008361)
5. Holloway Brooch – Museum of London, 1909 (Image 0013000)
6. Augustine Birrell – Author, Private Collection
7. Prince's Theatre – Author, Private Collection
8. Cicely Hamilton – by Miss Marie Leon (1867–?), facing page 41 of *A Pageant of Great Women* by Cicely Hamilton (London: The Suffrage Shop, 1910)
9. King George V in Bristol – Bristol Record Office, 4 July 1913 (Ref. No. 43207/9/11/8)
10. The burnt-out Sports Pavilion, *Daily Mirror* 26 October 1913 (University of Bristol Library, Special Collections)
11. Police view the WSPU shop – Bristol Record Office, c.1913 (Ref. No. 43207/22/19/20)
12. 'A is for Arson', *Nonesuch* 1913 – (University of Bristol Library, Special Collections)
13. Begbrook Mansion – Bristol Central Library
14. Eastville Park Boathouse – Bristol Record Office, 1910s (Ref. No. 43207/22/19/22)
15. 23 Gordon Road, Clifton – Michael Freeman, 2012
16. The Victoria Rooms, Clifton – Michael Freeman, 2012
17. The Coliseum, Park Row – Michael Freeman, 2012

Map photography by Michael Freeman, 2012

Bristol Suffragette Project

The aim of my Bristol Suffragette Project is to find out more about the Bristol suffragettes, suffragists and anti-suffragists. You can find out more about the project at www.lucienneboyce.com.

Was there a suffragette in your family? Have you got a suffragette story to tell or a local suffragette you'd like to include on the website? If you'd like to share your suffragette story you can email me at lucienne@lucienneboyce.com.

Endnotes

[1] WSPU Annual Report, 1907.

[2] Annie Kenney, *Memories of a Militant* (London: Edward Arnold & Co, 1924), p. 120.

[3] *Votes for Women*, 13 August 1908.

[4] *Western Daily Press*, Monday 21 September 1908.

[5] *Votes for Women*, 27 August 1908.

[6] *Votes for Women*, 22 October 1908.

[7] Emmeline Pankhurst, *My Own Story* (London: Virago, 1979), p. 119.

[8] Quoted in Antonia Raeburn, *Militant Suffragettes* (Newton Abbot: Victorian (& Modern History) Book Club, 1974; first published by Michael Joseph, 1973), p. 98.

[9] *Bristol Evening Post*, 9 September 1998.

[10] B.M. Willmott Dobbie, *A Nest of Suffragettes in Somerset* (The Batheaston Society, 1979), p. 38.

[11] *The Times*, 15 November 1909.

[12] *The Times*, 15 November 1909.

[13] *The Times*, 15 November 1909.

[14] Dobbie, p. 35.

[15] Roger Owen, *Lord Cromer: Victorian Imperialist, Edwardian Proconsul* (Oxford: Oxford University Press, 2004), p. 375.

[16] Edward David, ed., *Inside Asquith's Cabinet: From the Diaries of Charles Hobhouse* (London: Murray, 1977), p. 94.

[17] *Western Daily Press*, 17 February 1912.

[18] Pankhurst, *My Own Story*, p. 215.

[19] Pankhurst, *My Own Story*, p. 240.

[20] Sylvia Pankhurst, *The Suffragette Movement: An Intimate Account of Persons and Ideals* (London: Virago, 1977), p. 373.

[21] Pankhurst, *My Own Story*, p. 265.

[22] Pankhurst, *My Own Story*, p. 79.

[23] Pankhurst, *My Own Story*, p. 203.

[24] *Bristol Times and Mirror*, 27 June 1912.

[25] *The Daily Chronicle*, 25 October 1913.

[26] See letter dated 1 November 1913 to G. H. Pope Esq, J.P. in General Correspondence from the Principal 1911-19, Bristol Record Office, SMV/5/5/4/50.

[27] *The Suffragette*, 24 July 1914.

[28] Christabel Pankhurst, *Unshackled: The Story of How We Won the Vote* (London: Hutchinson, 1959), p. 288.

[29] Quoted in Pankhurst, *The Suffragette Movement*, p. 600.

[30] Dobbie, p. 38.

[31] *The Guardian*, 20 March 1908.
[32] *The Suffragette*, 23 May 1913.
[33] *The Times*, 11 March 1914.
[34] *The Suffragette*, 20 March 1914.

Index

Page numbers in italics refer to photos
WSPU = Women's Social and Political Union

"The militancy of men, through all the centuries, has drenched the world with blood, and for these deeds of horror and destruction men have been rewarded with monuments, with great songs and epics. The militancy of women has harmed no human life save the lives of those who fought the battle of righteousness. Time alone will reveal what reward will be allotted to women."

Christabel Pankhurst